Indochinese
Refugees
in America

Indochinese Refugees in America

Problems of

Adaptation and

Assimilation

Paul J. Strand

Woodrow Jones, Jr.

Duke Press Policy Studies

Duke University Press

Durham, North Carolina 1985

© 1985, Duke University Press
All rights reserved
Printed in the United States of America
Library of Congress Cataloging in Publication Data
Strand, Paul J., 1949–
Indochinese refugees in America.
(Duke Press policy studies)
Includes index.
1. Refugees—Indochina. 2. Refugees—United States.
3. Refugees—California. I. Jones, Woodrow. II. Title.
III. Series.
HV640.5.I5S77 1985 362.8'49592 84-25888
ISBN 0-8223-0629-8

Contents

Tables

Preface

The study that is described in this book grew out of a joint effort between the Social Science Research Laboratory (SSRL) of San Diego State University and ACCESS, a San Diego area private service provider that was contracted by the state of California to provide services to Indochinese refugees. The effort resulted in modest funding from the Regional Employment and Training Consortium for a needs assessment survey of San Diego area Indochinese refugees. The survey was conducted during the summer of 1981, the data were analyzed during the following winter, and a final report was submitted to the funding agency in March 1982.

I was encouraged by Professor Jones to pursue the study further, as the final report did not analyze all of the data that was provided by the survey. Unfortunately, the responsibility of directing a research laboratory required that new studies be given more immediate attention. A contract with Duke was not signed until 1983.

The completion of this book has depended on the efforts of many people. In the beginning, it was Lucy Lyons, Sandra Sveine, and Dr. Cuong Ngo-Anh who supervised the translation of the instrument, trained the interviewers, and supervised their fieldwork. They also assisted in the preparation of the final report. Later, Lawrence Sharp assisted Professor Jones and me in the preparation of two health-related articles, and David Mills assisted me in the preparation of an employment article.

Research for much of the background material included in the first section of the book was conducted by Jeanne Frey and Andrew

Isbell. Finally, the completion of the manuscript has depended on the exhaustive efforts of Carole Outhouse. She managed the typing and informed the authors of omissions and deletions. She and all other participants mentioned above were employed by the SSRL. Without the contribution of SSRL, the project could not have been completed.

We hope the information provided in the following pages will assist those involved in the resettlement of Indochinese refugees so that the exigency of their resettlement can be managed. The San Diego area refugee community was very cooperative in this study and the experience of dealing with them enlightening. Their situation deserves attention.

Paul J. Strand
Woodrow Jones, Jr.

1
Immigrants, Refugees, and Resettlement

During the first half of the twentieth century mass population movements tended to be *voluntary* migrations. During the second half, *involuntary* migrations became a significant factor in these movements. Modern refugee movements have given rise to a new class of people who are homeless and stateless and who live in a condition of constant stress and insecurity. The problems of reception, administration, and resettlement of these refugees have taxed and overloaded governmental institutions, and created many other political and socioeconomic problems for host societies.

Although refugees were once considered a temporary phenomenon, their increasing numbers have required governments, private agencies, and other international organizations to cooperate in finding solutions to what is now seen as an ongoing problem. Several national governments have already created permanent agencies to coordinate resettlement activities. In the United States, the Office of Refugee Resettlement (ORR) was created by the Refugee Act of 1980. The discussions that led to the passage of this act reflected a growing recognition that the focus of United States immigration policy cannot be restricted to the problems that occur along the United States–Mexico border. The diversity of transnational population movements requires new policies that are effective in coordinating the resettlement of many different groups of immigrants.

The chapters in this book focus on the context and experiences of Indochinese refugees who resettled in the United States after the Vietnam War. The United States has taken a large share of the responsibility of resettling refugees who were forced to migrate due to the fall of the government of South Vietnam and the subsequent actions of the new government. In the following pages we examine the policies and experiences of resettling these refugees and evaluate their adaptation to American society.

These refugees are not typical of most other immigrants to the United States. They have dissimilar cultures, experiences, and expectations. Furthermore, their migration is neither voluntary nor economic. It is forced by a fear of retaliation and repression. Their numbers and their conditions upon arrival are certain to strain the adaptability of American society. Our examination is aimed at the problems of adaptation in one resettlement site.

The Conditions of Refugee Migration

Before examining the details of Indochinese migration, it may be useful to examine the general conditions of refugee migration. Traditionally, migrants are viewed as people in a social unit who decide to solve problems through mobility.[1] The decision to migrate implies a degree of blockage in the pursuit of social and economic goals. Migrants must feel that some needs or desires are not being adequately fulfilled in their present location. These feelings are always relative: they require the *perception* of inadequate means of acquiring satisfaction of wants and needs.[2]

Certainly, this definition of transnational migration and immigration assumes the freedom of choice in the migration decision. In the context of political upheaval, refugee migrations have been considered a special category of transnational migrations. The political refugee relocates because of the threats of political persecution. The relocation is largely involuntary.[3] The term "forced migration" has been used as a description of this special class of migrants. In conditions of forced migration, migrants do not retain any "power to decide whether or not to leave."[4] "It is the reluctance to uproot oneself, and the absence of positive motivations to settle elsewhere, which characterize all refugee decisions and distinguish this refugee from the voluntary migrant."[5]

The characteristics of forced migration present problems for host societies. These population movements have been noted as being rapid and without adequate preparation.[6] Often the host society and the migrant population do not have the resources necessary for successful resettlement. Basic resources such as money and the acquisition of language and employment skills become the burden of the international community. Furthermore, forced migrations are often connected with a controlling government which directs their movement and exodus for political reasons. Upon arrival, social and cultural differences between the migrants and host societies play a critical role in shaping the migrants' resettlement experiences. Deepseated mistrust and fear of authority are impediments to adapting to the new environment.

In sum, forced migration is different from any other government-influenced migration. The voluntary political refugee sees the migration as a means of escaping political oppression and the establishment of a new way of life. The forced migrants, on the other hand, have an orientation toward the retention of the past and not a reorientation toward the new. These refugees lack the motivation to migrate and, since their movement is not voluntary, they experience a sense of powerlessness which hampers their assimilation into a new society.

Global Responses to Forced Migration

The pattern of forced migration has been toward the western hemisphere, with refugees more likely to concentrate in the industrialized countries of Western Europe, Canada, and the United States. Since government policies vary as to the definition of a refugee, many refugees do not attain an actual refugee status and are, at best, considered quasi-refugees. This situation is complicated by refugee perceptions that international assistance will make the possibility of resettlement in an industrialized nation a reality.

The definitional problems of refugee status prevent recognition of the true nature of the migration. For instance, most liberal nations require the presence of "barriers to exit" for the designation of a political refugee. The increasing number of arrivals from the People's Republic of China in Hong Kong has resulted in "the paradoxical spectacle of a free country demanding of a totalitarian one to impose more effective barriers."[7] By foreclosing to them the alternative of voting with their feet, liberal countries, in effect, contribute to the maintenance of authoritarian regimes.

The United Nations has played a key role in defining the problems of refugees and in developing cooperative strategies for resettling displaced populations. The United Nations High Commission for Refugees (UNHCR), established by the United Nations in 1951, is the major agency for working with refugees. The original mission of UNHCR was to protect refugees from the crisis and aftermath of World War II. Since then, it has become a major actor in coordinating international funds for refugee assistance. However, the present large flow of refugees has led to the development of doubts about the capacity of the international community to respond to the problems of forced migrations.[8]

The limitations in the United Nations' effort have been the lack of adequate international funds to meet the demands of rapid migration and the identification of national funds for finding a permanent solution to a refugee crisis. The UNHCR primarily contracts with other agencies to carry out its mandate. Although its budget has grown exponentially during the last thirty years, this growth has not matched the needs of the growing refugee population. Other agencies such as UNICEF, the International Commission on Migration (ICM), and various regional bodies provide supplemental support for refugee assistance. Most international support is geared toward the medical needs of the refugees while general resettlement support remains the responsibility of the nation of final asylum.

International relief funding comes mainly from the governments of the industrialized nations. Since the refugee crisis has international political consequences, most governments prefer to offer funding through multinational organizations. Thus, the UNHCR receives most of its funds from the United States, Great Britain, West Germany, Japan, France, and Canada.

There are a number of private relief organizations that supplement the international apparatus for the assisting of refugees. The Lutheran World Federation, the World Council of Churches, Catholic groups, and other missionary groups in Third World countries provide much of the manpower and aid for the resettlement of refugees. These religious organizations are supplemented by private secular voluntary agencies such as the League of Red Cross Societies and the International Committee of the Red Cross. Their efforts, unlike those of governments, have focused on the long-term effect of migration on the refugee and the society of asylum.

Government relief funds have focused on two aspects of the international refugee crisis. First, they have focused on the impact that a massive influx of refugees has on Third World countries. These nations often become sites of temporary asylum where care and sheltering of the refugee is dependent upon funds from international relief agencies. Second, government relief funds have focused on the permanent resettlement of refugees. The country of permanent asylum has the responsibility for providing the refugee with temporary assistance in order to ease the pain of migration. Thus, government relief assistance has been geared toward short-term assistance but not long-term resettlement aid.

In summation, the international apparatus for the assistance of refugees involves three sets of institutions working simultaneously to provide a solution to the crisis created by forced migration. Governments direct their efforts toward immigration policy and short-range solutions to enable permanent asylum. Voluntary agencies provide assistance for both temporary and long-term resettlement needs. And international relief agencies provide the international funding and coordination of relief assistance.

Indochinese and International Migration

As the following chapter indicates, the Indochinese migration meets all the requirements of a forced migration. The rapid movement of Vietnamese during the fall of Saigon and the later flights by sea were involuntary. In addition, fears of reprisal as well as intense shelling "pushed" many Cambodian, Laotian, and Hmong migrants across their borders into Thailand. Temporary refugee camps were established along these borders and in other Asian nations to respond to the immediate needs of these new migrants.

The world community responded with hesitancy toward the possibility of resettling such a large number of refugees. Despite the worldwide attention given to incidents in which "boat people" were being turned back to sea, only a few countries were willing to accept appreciable numbers of these refugees for resettlement. By the end of 1979 there were more than 14,000 land refugees in thirteen camps in Thailand and more than 75,000 boat refugees in one Malaysia camp. Malaysia saw these refugees, many of whom were ethnic Chinese, as disrupting the delicate Malay-Chinese racial balance. Thailand viewed the refugees as upsetting the delicate political balance between the new governments of Vietnam, Laos, and Cambodia.[9]

Other nations expressed similar political concerns about the possibility of resettling a large number of refugees. Indonesian officials expressed concern about the impact of overcrowding on its social problems. Hong Kong officials voiced strong opposition to the influx of more refugees, given the number of refugees coming from the People's Republic of China. Similar doubts were expressed by a number of countries, including those offering first asylum.[10]

In an effort to attain worldwide participation in the resettlement effort, the UNHCR coordinated several conferences to solicit the support of industrialized nations. It also provided financing for the temporary care of refugees. The asylum country governments and voluntary agencies were responsible for providing the organization for the delivery of aid. Unfortunately, worldwide support for this effort has been lacking, and criticism of the ineptness of first asylum countries in providing for basic necessities in refugee camps has mounted.

As table 1.1 indicates, the patterns of resettlement of Indochinese refugees have generally reflected the dominant actors in Indochina's history, with the United States and France assuming the bulk of responsibility. The long history of French involvement and the recent history of American involvement appear to be important factors in their willingness to accept these large numbers. Other nations, such as Australia and Canada, were motivated by humanitarian concern, as well as pressure from Western allies.

Overall, departures to the United States represent over half of the Indochinese departures from countries of first asylum. Still there are estimates of over 300,000 refugees in camps awaiting immigration and resettlement in countries of permanent asylum. With the possibility of more refugees, many Western nations have developed national refugee policies to meet this contingency and to meet the needs of countries which are now sites of temporary asylum.

Policy Issues Underlying Refugees and Resettlement

The burden of support for the immigration and resettlement of Indochinese refugees has had a disproportionate impact on the host society. Social problems have been numerous but have generally been surmounted through the coordination of immigration and social welfare policies. However, four major social problems have had recurring effects on the nature of the resettlement experience of involuntary refugees.

First, the size of the flow of all types of refugees is not currently controllable, and therefore does not allow for an orderly transition into the country of permanent asylum. Many have argued that immigration policies that inhibit mass migration are necessary to protect social structures from the shock effects of involuntary migration.[11] In the case of the Indochinese refugees, there has been mounting internal criticism of the United States' ability to maintain high admission programs for this group given the large number of refugees from other areas such as Africa.[12] Questions regarding migrant workers and undocumented aliens further complicate this issue. The magnitude of the social strain that lies ahead is not addressed by current U.S. refugee policy.

Second, social criticism has mounted over the allocation of societal resources to these refugees, and over their refugee classification. It has been suggested that a large proportion of these refugees have been motivated by "pull" factors such as economic betterment rather than "push" factors such as political persecution. For example, many of the refugees who have recently arrived in the United States have had little contact with the United States' efforts in the Vietnam War. In addition, upon arrival, many of these refugees have been accused of abusing social welfare services and exploiting social programs. This is especially bothersome given the high cost of resettling refugees in a period when many such social programs are being reduced.

Third, the level of support for the resettlement of these refugees has set a precedent for future refugees. Criticism within the United States has been directed at this level of support and the burden it has placed on state governments. Some states have borne an unfair burden in becoming prime sites for resettlement of large refugee populations. With other nations reducing their refugee flows, the United States is absorbing larger proportions of recent refugees. These recent arrivals tend to resettle in established sites due to family connections and the presence of a developed resettlement infrastructure. Thus, states with large enclaves of refugees are now experiencing population growths which place further burdens on social welfare programs.

Finally, there is concern over the effectiveness of resettlement

Table 1.1   Indochinese refugee activity April 1975 through June 1981

Countries of asylum/RPC's	Total addition since 1975 Arrivals
Hong Kong	101,569
Macau	7,099
Indonesia	66,218
Japan	4,999
Malaysia	158,748
Philippines	21,524
Singapore	23,832
Thailand	62,590
Other	31,472
Total boat	478,051
Thailand-Khmer	211,648
Thailand-Hmong	123,267
Thailand-Lao	145,000[a]
Thailand-Vietnamese	21,370[b]
Total land	501,285
Orderly Departure Program	3,230
Vietnam to U.S. in 1975	124,547
Vietnam to China in 1975	263,000
Total direct	390,777
Bataan-RPC	44,556
Galang-RPC	15,677
Total RPC's	60,233
Grand total	1,370,113

a. Thai Ministry of Interior census at Nong Khai camp reduced its population by 1,022 Lao refugees who had left camp earlier, but who had not been removed from camp rolls. Actually about 1,600 new Lao refugees entered the UNHCR/MOI camp system during June 1981 and are destined for the Nakhom Phanom holding center.

b. This is a UNHCR mathematically derived figure. No land Vietnamese have been permitted to enter camp NW-9 on the Thai-Kampuchean border for the

		Total reductions since April 1975			
Other	To U.S.	3rd countries	Voluntary repatriation	Other	RPC's
891	39,752	43,035	0	146	4,674
57	1,915	2,328	0	549	788
33	37,626	22,974	0	4	106
19	2,414	972	0	0	0
109	78,649	60,677	0	9	4,000
16	7,909	5,463	0	3	2,929
2	4,363	13,845	1	0	2,177
0	21,853	14,779	0	0	11,852
5	2,632	28,434	0	0	0
1,132	197,113	192,507	1	711	26,526
0	29,891	33,281	0	0	18,561
0	47,790	19,469	18	0	77
0	61,737	26,729	245		11,469
0	7,013	8,709	0	0	3,381
0	146,431	88,188	263	0	33,515
0	2,341	875	0	14	0
0	123,000	0	1,547[c]	0	0
0	0	263,000	0	0	0
0	125,341	263,875	1,547[c]	14	0
440	27,200	637	0	11	
115	7,821	972	0	2	82
555	35,021	1,609	0	13	82
1,687	503,906	546,179	1,811	724	60,137

last two months. These are the UNHCR's revised estimates on the total number of land Vietnamese refugees in camp and increased its total number of land Vietnamese already in the centers by 2,378.

c. All returned from Guam in 1975 on ship *(Thuongh Tin I)* to Vietnam; several dozens have since fled Vietnam by boat beginning in early 1979.

Note: RPC arrivals are not included in the arrival grand total because it would result in double addition. Departures to RPC's are not subtracted across grand total line because it would result in double subtraction.

Source: U.S., House of Representatives, Committee on the Judiciary, *Refugee Admission Proposal,* Hearing, 97th Cong., 1st Sess., 29 September 1981 (Washington: Government Printing Office, 1981), 112.

programs. The conceptualization and implementation of resettlement programs vary from nation to nation. And, within the United States there is variation from state to state regarding how programs should be designed and implemented to attain the goals of assimilation and self-sufficiency. These issues are compounded by the role conflicts between state and local authorities and voluntary agencies. Furthermore, there are many other issues, including the racial, social, and physiological stresses that affect the refugee population. These stresses are factors in the refugees' ability to assimilate and adapt to American life.

Conclusion

The problems associated with the involuntary migration and adaptation of Indochinese refugees is the focal point of this book. The book examines the experiences of this group of involuntary migrants and gives an overview of the key issues and problems underlying U.S. resettlement policies. Compared with other fields in the study of international movements, the field of refugee resettlement is only recently emerging. Thus, this study should further our knowledge of the consequences of immigration policies toward refugees. It will also provide a detailed analysis of the social adjustment of Indochinese refugees in one American community.

The historical pattern of resettlement in the United States has been established by the experiences of European immigrants who arrived at the turn of the century. First the immigrant population adapts economically but not socially. With time, a slow process of acculturation and adaptation is accomplished through education.[13] But this pattern of assimilation has not as accurately characterized Asian ethnic groups or involuntary migrants. These migrants have special problems in accepting and adapting to a society they do not prefer. This book provides much-needed information on the adjustment of these refugees to American culture.

This book is divided into three sections. The first section provides a synthesis of information on the backgrounds of these refugees and on government policies and programs that have been designed to alleviate resettlement barriers. The purpose of this section is to provide an overview of the policy setting in which all local policy makers operate and through which the refugees must assimilate.

The second section of the book examines Indochinese refugees as individuals who face resettlement problems related to day-to-day living, language, health, and employment. The examination is unique in that it covers the differential impacts of resettlement on each refugee ethnic group. The context for the examination is a large refugee community in southern California.

The final section of the book offers an assessment and policy recommendations. The set of policy recommendations offered in the last chapter of the book is based on previous analysis and on this examination of the experiences of these refugees. We hope that this effort will assist in providing the empirical and analytical resources necessary to implement policies that will ease the pain of this resettlement and the resettlement of other groups of refugees which are almost certain to seek asylum in the future.

2
Prearrival Experiences

Since the fall of Saigon over 600,000 Indochinese refugees have entered the United States. These refugees, from five major ethnic groups, represent a new kind of migrant population. They include Vietnamese, ethnic Chinese from Vietnam, ethnic Lao and Hmong from Laos, and Khmer from Cambodia. All of them come from cultures very different from that of the earlier, predominantly European immigrant. Many of them have spent years as displaced persons within their own countries, their traditional ways of life altered by the effects of devastating wars and aid-dependent economies. This chapter describes the traditional cultural backgrounds of these refugees, the historical and political events that led to the collapse of U.S.-supported regimes in this area, and their subsequent flight and resettlement in the United States and other countries.

The countries that constitute former French Indochina present a diversity of ethnic groups and cultural traditions. The ethnic Lao, Khmer, and Vietnamese are dominant politically and economically in their respective countries. These lowland delta peoples have a long tradition of state-level political organization and contact with the "Great Traditions" of India and China. There are also many hill tribes such as the Hmong. These are primarily slash and burn, or swidden, farmers with village-level political organization. Finally, Southeast Asia, in particular Vietnam, is also home to the largest overseas population of ethnic Chinese, with nearly five-sixths of the total overseas Chinese population.[1]

Geography plays a major role in the diversity of these groups.

The most important geographic feature is the separation of high-lands from lowlands. An extension of the Himalayas, the Indo-Malayan mountain chain, curves through the Indochinese peninsula and separates the Tonkin Delta region of northern Vietnam from the Mekong Delta, the plains of Cambodia, and the lowlands of south-ern Laos. This also marks a major cultural separation. North Viet-nam has been within the Chinese sphere of influence for over two thousand years and was a Chinese province for much of that time. The southern areas, on the other hand, have been influenced by contact with India. These distinctive cultural influences have re-sulted in very different social structures and world views.

The lowlands, fed by the Mekong River in the south and the Song-Koi (Red River) in the north, have provided a fertile environ-ment for rice farming. Rice is by far the most important economic resource and commodity in this region. Prior to the escalation of the war in the mid-1960s, over 80 percent of the population in these areas were rural farmers. Much of the retail activities, and nearly all the rice trade, was controlled by the Chinese.

The highland people are mainly swidden farmers. They gener-ally have little or no political organization more complex than the village. The ruggedness of the mountains and the poor navigability of the Mekong and Song-Koi rivers have contributed to the isolation and diversity of the ethnic groups that populate the highlands. Laos has over fifty of these groups, with the lowland ethnic Lao forming less than half the population. Hill tribes are generally regarded by the lowland peoples as backward and ignorant. In Laos, the former Royal Lao Government did little to incorporate these tribes into the political process. The Pathet Lao were the first to make a concerted effort to secure their support.

The Lao and Laos

There is great respect for age and authority among the Lao. Property is equally divided among sons and daughters. This tendency toward wide dispersion of property within a few generations is compensated for by preferential second cousin marriage, restricting the set of kinsmen.[2] Individuals are seen as being inextricably imbedded in a web of relationships that center on the family and community. Ethnic diversity, lack of development, and rugged terrain have impeded the development of a sense of national identity. Most Lao lack a sense of themselves as members of a Lao nation, as the village is probably the largest social and political unit to which one's sense of belonging and loyalty extends.

The Lao culture is dominated by the traditions and ideology of Buddhism, a religion that is also responsible for the formal education of young Lao and Khmer males. Buddhism begins with the notion of worldly impermanence. All things are composed of different elements, and everything is in a constant state of flux. Since all things are constituent and constantly changing, the ego, or individual self, has no real existence. Ignorance of the true state of the world leads to desires for permanence, material things, and attachments to people. Desires or cravings result in sorrow, or *dukkha*, which can only be alleviated by following the Eightfold Path, living a moderate life of discipline, moral conduct, concentration, and meditation.

Although there is no individual self in Buddhism, there is a soul which transmigrates. One continues to be reborn until Nirvana, a state of nonego, is attained. The cycle of rebirth can be affected by one's actions, positive or negative. This law of karma is a kind of cosmic accounting, the effects of one's actions extending into the future. Ritualized "acts of merit" are possible, to counter the effects of negative karma and to accumulate good karma for the future.

Popular religious practice also includes a great many animist beliefs. Though ultimate causation is attributed to the principle of karma, many events are blamed on an assortment of spirits, ghosts, and demons. There also exist ritual specialists in these groups with no connection to Buddhism.

In terms of its political boundaries, Laos is a creation of the French. Its borders were established by several treaties that used the Mekong River to separate it from Thailand.[3] These treaties left the ethnic Lao forming less than half the population of Laos, with considerably more Lao residing in Thailand.[4] Nevertheless, ethnic Lao are the political and economic élite of Laos.

The primary economic activity in Laos is wet-rice agriculture. More than 80 percent of Laos is rural subsistence agricultural villages. All productive property and family labor is collectively owned and used by the household, under the supervision of the family head, usually the senior male. There is usually a sexual division of labor in Laos, men doing most of the heavy agricultural labor and hunting, women being responsible for domestic tasks. Economic development in Laos has been minimal. The French, who occupied Laos for so many years, invested very little in terms of personnel, transportation facilities, education, or health care.[5]

The Japanese occupied Laos during World War II. Following their defeat, Laotian independence was declared by Prince Phetserath. This lasted only a short time, as the French reoccupied Laos in 1946. It was not until 1953 that the Geneva accords established Laotian independence under the Royal Lao government. However, a 1949 split in the party that formed the exiled post–World War II government resulted in the creation of the Progressive Peoples Organization, forerunner of the Pathet Lao and ally of the Viet Minh. By the time the Royal Lao government came to power in 1953, the Pathet Lao had gained control of over half of the Lao countryside.

The Geneva Conference recognized the importance of the Pathet Lao, giving them two northeastern provinces as "regroupment zones." It also recognized the need for the integration of the Pathet Lao with the Royal Lao government, but did not specify how this was to be accomplished.

The first such effort began in 1956. This effort gave Pathet Lao members several government posts, and the two northeastern provinces were turned over to the Royal Lao government (although the Pathet Lao retained most administrative functions). Concern in the United States about the influence of the Pathet Lao led to a suspension of U.S. aid in 1958, forcing the collapse of the coalition government, the rise to power of rightist factions, and increased conflict.

U.S. perceptions of the military threat posed by the Pathet Lao resulted in greatly increased military aid under the guise of a civilian Program Evaluations Office. This response indicated inexperience with the type of guerrilla warfare the Royal Lao government was facing.[6] The Royal Lao Army was transformed into a miniature model of U.S. conventional forces, with the United States providing the entire military budget. Little attention was paid to counterguerrilla tactics, and the army was made up of lowland Lao exclusively. In contrast, the Pathet Lao were based in the villages, had made a concentrated effort to involve ethnic minorities, and provided superior organization and administration.

Following the collapse of the coalition government in 1958, there was escalation of the guerrilla war and the increasing involvement of the North Vietnamese. Laos became of major strategic importance to the North Vietnamese as a supply line to their forces in South Vietnam. This supply line, the Ho Chi Minh trail, ran the length of eastern Laos, through rugged mountains, continuing down into Cambodia.

A new agreement, signed in Geneva in 1962, provided for the neutrality of Laos and again attempted to establish a coalition government. 1962 also marked the beginning of the secret war in Laos, the CIA creating a Hmong counterguerrilla force based in the high mountains around the Plain of Jars. Again the coalition failed. A rightist coup in 1964 forced the Pathet Lao back into the jungles.

A massive escalation of the U.S. presence in Indochina also began in 1964. Bombing raids against the Ho Chi Minh trail increased to more than 12,500 a month. The Plain of Jars was virtually depopulated, and 150,000 people were displaced. By 1970, two-thirds of Laos had been bombed. The bombing created more than 600,000 refugees, over 20 percent of the total population of Laos. The refugee flow increased at a rate faster than they could be resettled.[7] By 1973 the United States was providing food for 378,000 of these refugees.[8]

Another attempt at a coalition government was made, following a 1973 ceasefire, in 1974. By 1975 this coalition also began to collapse. Rightists in the government provoked a Pathet Lao military reaction by moving Vang Pao's Hmong troops into a region of unrest and by devaluing the Lao currency. The Pathet Lao were better organized politically, and moved to consolidate their position. By 23 May 1975, four out of five rightist government ministers and a number of military leaders resigned and fled the country, as did many other wealthy Lao residents, including large numbers of Vietnamese and Chinese merchants.[9]

Hmong

The Hmong are representative of the tribal hill peoples of Southeast Asia. They have gained particular recognition for their role as guerrilla fighters in Laos, operating with U.S. clandestine support from bases in the mountains surrounding the strategic Plain of Jars.[10] They have a high degree of ethnic identity and political and social solidarity.[11] There are perhaps as many as three million Hmong distributed across southern China and the mountainous northern regions of Southeast Asia, of which 300,000–400,000 are in Laos, where they constitute 10 percent of the population. They prefer to live above 3,000 feet elevation, and are highly migratory.[12] In 1959 there were an estimated 45,000 living in the area around the Plain of Jars.[13] This group, due to their long involvement with the U.S. war in Laos against the Pathet Lao, have become a target of persecution by the Pathet Lao following their takeover in 1975.

Hmong are slash and burn farmers. The importance of opium poppy cultivation as a cash crop leads to rapid soil depletion. The depletion of their soil forces the Hmong to migrate in search of new land to cultivate. This migratory cycle usually occurs in ten-year intervals. The cultivation and sale of opium has affected the productive relations of the Hmong and made them wealthier than most other hill tribes.[14] It has also kept them more involved in political events and tied them economically to a cash-based market economy.

Hmong are patrilineal, having corporate lineages and clan-level organization. These provide kinship links which facilitate the movement to new areas. Although the lineage does have ritual significance, the main social linkages are those between brothers and their families and their fathers' brothers and their families. The household is the basic social and productive unit. These are generally nuclear or stem families, though large extended families are also common.

The Hmong are divided into a number of clans. Clans differ primarily in certain ritual practices, and are "essentially religious associations conferring rights of community upon their members through the spiritual bonds between them."[15] The characteristic style and color of a Hmong woman's dress is used to distinguish one clan from another (although other characteristics may be used as well).

Clans recruit new members principally through the bringing in of women, as wives, from other clans. Their children will be members of the father's clan, the males retaining membership in the same clan throughout their lives, the females leaving to become members of their husband's clan upon marriage. If a woman leaves her husband's clan, either because of his death or in cases of divorce, the clan is entitled to compensation for the loss.

Clans are widely dispersed, do not come together in assembly, and lack political organization. They aid in migration by providing ties to individuals in other areas and by acting as mutual aid associations. Most important locally are the unnamed subclans, which are distinguished by certain differences in ritual practices. Subclans may actively invite other subclan members to resettle, providing them with land whenever possible.

The household is the primary social and economic unit. Subsistence productive property is held in common, under the control of the household head, who is usually the senior male. Respect for age is emphasized and personal leadership qualities are important. Productive property and labor concerned with cash cropping are separate, the family of each married son controlling its own wealth. This may lead to internal conflicts over the allocation of resources.[16] Households are subject to frequent splitting, one married son or brother taking his family and resettling in a new area. Often he will encourage other household members to resettle in this same area where they will form new separate households. The separation of cash activities from subsistence activities allows each family a measure of independence which eases the process of migration and resettlement.[17]

The village is the largest political unit for the Hmong. Leadership is provided by the headman, who is usually a member of the dominant clan in the village. He is selected by consensus, on the basis of individual qualities and ability. Most of his duties consist of arbitration of village disputes. In these he must promote consensus and act as the spokesman for the community. He also is the village representative to the larger political community.

In 1961 the U.S. Army Special Forces began to equip and train a force of about nine thousand Hmong under the guise of the White Star Mobile Training Teams.[18] In addition, nearly one hundred Thai advisors were stationed with the Hmong. For the Hmong, the war was a conflict that involved rival clans. The CIA-backed forces were loyal to Touby Lyfong, a member of the Ly clan and an important Hmong leader. Faydang, a leader of the rival Lo clan, allied himself with the Pathet Lao after losing a leadership battle to Lyfong.

The clans loyal to Lyfong were commanded by Vang Pao, who had begun his fight against the Viet Minh in 1945 with the Free French Forces. The Hmong counterguerrillas proved very effective, using tactics similar to those of the Pathet Lao. Following the collapse of the coalition government in 1975, the Pathet Lao began a genocidal campaign against the Hmong. In May 1975 the official Pathet Lao newspaper announced that the "Meo (Hmong) must be exterminated."[19] By 1978 it was estimated that nearly 10 percent of the Hmong had been killed. In the wake of this effort, many of the Hmong fled to Thailand.

As of late February 1983 there were 76,000 refugees from Laos in Thai camps. Nearly three-quarters of these were highland tribal people, predominantly Hmong. The first wave of refugees came following the Pathet Lao victory in 1975. A second wave came in 1979. Lao refugees constituted 47 percent of Thailand's total refugee population. Many had been resettled by 1981 when Thailand introduced a "human deterrence" policy that banned the resettlement of lowland Lao. The policy was later expanded to include Vietnamese and highland tribal people as well.

The Khmer

The Khmer are members of the Mon-Khmer language family, whereas the Lao are Thai speakers of the Sino-Tibetan language family. The Khmer are a majority group, constituting about 85 percent of the population of Cambodia, with ethnic Chinese and Vietnamese constituting over 10 percent. In many other respects, the Lao and Khmer are members of a general Theravada Buddhist lowland culture. They have similar kinship systems, animist beliefs, modes of production, and world view.

The Khmer state was one of the great civilizations of Southeast Asia, centered in the royal city of Angkor. This empire lasted from 802 to 1432 A.D. before collapsing into a state of vassalage to both the Vietnamese kingdom in Cochinchina and the Siamese. It remained a vassal state until the French, claiming the Vietnamese rights in Cambodia as part of its prerogatives as a colonial power in Cochinchina, took control of the area in 1863. As in Laos, the French ruled indirectly, utilizing native authority wherever possible. French colonial rule did not go unchallenged. There was a serious rebellion in 1866–67, led by Pon Kombo and tacitly supported by the king, which required as many as 10,000 French troops to restore order. In 1916 as many as 100,000 peasants demonstrated against the French in Phnom Penh.[20]

The ancient Khmer kingdom was a theocratic state and the

former king, Prince Norodom Sihanouk, is still seen by many of the Khmer as a god-king. Much of Sihanouk's popularity among the peasants and his ability to continue to survive as a viable political actor rest upon this aura of religiously sanctioned power, part of the long historical and cultural tradition of the area.[21] This has enabled Sihanouk to survive a number of unlikely political alliances, such as the present tripartite resistance government opposing the Vietnamese-backed government of Heng Samrin.

Sihanouk, as King of Cambodia, declared Cambodian independence in March 1944. Son Ngoc Thanh, a conservative who was to play a continuing role in opposing Sihanouk, was named Minister of Foreign Affairs. Thanh attempted a coup and assumed the premiership. He was arrested by French and British authorities and exiled.

In 1946 Cambodia was declared an autonomous state within the French Union. This was independence in name only, as French advisors remained and the approval of the French Commissioner was required for all laws and regulations. In 1947 Prince Yutevong wrote a constitution modeled directly on the French Republic and formed the Democratic Party, composed primarily of the urban élite, who were rightist-monarchists.

Sihanouk dissolved the national assembly in 1949 and formed a new government in 1951 which he again dissolved in 1952, naming himself prime minister of the new government. Thanh had returned from exile in 1952 to oppose Sihanouk, and was again exiled. Thanh returned again in 1955 as the Democratic Party candidate. Sihanouk, moving to counter the influence of the Democratic Party, abdicated and formed the People's Socialist Community, a mass-based political movement. He won the elections and retained the prime ministership. Thanh was exiled to South Vietnam where he formed a CIA-backed rightist guerrilla army.

The attempt by Sihanouk to maintain Cambodian neutrality and to preserve his own political position from attacks by both the left and the right proved impossible in the long run, given the increasing intensity of the war in Vietnam and U.S. pressure. During the elections of 1962–63 the secret police arrested hundreds of intellectuals, forcing some into the jungles where they began to develop the infrastructure of the Khmer Rouge resistance movement.

In 1963 Sihanouk nationalized the import/export trade and the banks, and began to refuse U.S. aid. The economy began to worsen and Sihanouk was forced to rely increasingly on Russian and Chinese aid. He also increased ties with the Viet Minh and National Liberation Front (NLF), allowing them free use of Cambodia for passage of men and materials, and as a sanctuary. Informal agreements with the NLF and the North Vietnamese were concluded in 1965, and formal recognition was granted to the Provisional Revolutionary Government in 1969. In response, the United States increased its border incursions and began intensive bombing of the eastern provinces. The United States also began defoliation of the countryside. In May 1969 the United States defoliated nearly 40,000 acres of Cambodian rubber trees, one-third of its total.[22]

In March 1970, with the approval of the United States, General Lon Nol and a group of rightists seized power in Cambodia. The Lon Nol government immediately broke off relations with the North Vietnamese, Viet Minh, and Provisional Revolutionary Government. The United States was given a free hand in Cambodia, and greatly intensified its activities. Between 1970 and 1975 the United States dropped half a million tons of bombs on heavily populated areas, creating over 3 million refugees.[23] The population of Phnom Penh tripled as refugees fled the destruction. By 1975 it had grown to over three million people.

The Lon Nol government was a repressive one, and public protest grew increasingly violent. This allowed the Khmer Rouge to greatly extend their control of the countryside. Sihanouk formed the Khmer National Unified Front and supported armed insurrection against Lon Nol. Prior to their victory, and after a purge of Sihanouk supporters, the Khmer Rouge controlled 80 percent of Cambodia. The fall of the Lon Nol government came rapidly. On 17 April 1975 the Khmer Rouge entered Phnom Penh.

The repressive government of Lon Nol was replaced by a reign of terror that shocked the world when details finally surfaced. Driven by a fanatical distrust of the cities and the belief in the impossibility of reforming the élite, intellectuals, and anyone associated with the former regime, the Khmer Rouge under Pol Pot murdered millions of people. Within several days they had evacuated all urban areas, including the 3 million residents of Phnom Penh. The population was relocated to the countryside where they were immediately put to work. Many died during the relocation or in the famine that followed. Between September and December 1975 a second forced relocation led to the deaths of many more Khmer, who could not survive the effects of famine, lack of medical care, and malaria.[24] Many intellectuals and government officials fled. More than 150,000 entered Vietnam, and more than 33,000 entered Thailand.

In 1978 Vietnam, now under the control of the Communists, invaded Cambodia, replacing the Pol Pot government with a puppet government under Heng Samrin. An additional 100,000 Cambodians, fearing the traditional animosity between the Vietnamese and Khmer, fled to Thailand. A third wave, driven by continuing famine and Vietnamese offensives, formed refugee camps, in the face of resistance, along the Thai-Cambodian border. This third wave numbered nearly 500,000. International relief efforts, better rice harvests, and the stability of the Samrin government led to a decrease in this flow of refugees. Close to 300,000 remain in Thailand and along the border areas, 94,000 in Thai holding centers, and 200,000 in border camps under the control of the three Cambodian resistance factions. These three have formed a coalition resistance government.[25]

There are also about 30,000 Cambodian refugees, most of them ethnic Chinese, in Vietnam.[26] Some 14,000 of these are living in camps set up with the help of the United Nations High Commissioner for Refugees (UNHCR). Another 10,000 are in Saigon.

Despite a locally high tax rate, the French invested little in Cambodia's economic development. French neglect in Cambodia is illustrated by the fact that, by 1939, only four Cambodians had graduated from senior high school. By 1941 there were only 537 secondary school students out of a population of nearly three million people. Cambodia also has had one of the highest infant mortality rates and highest rates of illiteracy in Southeast Asia.[27]

Cambodia, more so than Laos or Vietnam, has been primarily a nation of small independent landowner farmers. However, by 1930, over half the land was owned by the wealthiest 20 percent of farmers. By 1950, four-fifths of the peasants owned only enough land to achieve minimal subsistence levels of production.[28] By 1970, 20 percent of the farmers were tenants. Due to high interest rates, 75 percent of the peasants were in serious debt by 1952. In addition, the rural economy was fragmented, composed mostly of autonomous village households with no communal lands or community organizations.

The general character of social and political interaction is strongly conditioned by Buddhist moral and ethical teachings which stress respect, a lack of argumentativeness and willingness to compromise, consensus, and a social face of serenity and passivity. The teachings also discourage the conspicuous accumulation of wealth, power, or prestige.[29]

Vietnamese

Vietnam was more developed by the French than either Laos or Cambodia. The French introduced rubber plantations in the south, over 90 percent of which were French-owned. The plantations used indebted Vietnamese peasants for labor. Land tenancy patterns began to shift, particularly in the south, and the percentage of landless tenant farmers grew rapidly.[30] There emerged a wealthy, French-educated, landowning élite. In the Tonkin area the French developed extractive industries, and there began to develop an industrial working class. The French also held a monopoly on salt, alcohol, and opium. Commercial development required an infrastructure, and the French made extensive use of corvée labor in the construction of railroads and highways. As a result of French modernization of agriculture, rice production increased. However, because of French exploitation, actual consumption of rice declined, the increase in production being exported rather than consumed. Another consequence of exploitation was the development of a dual economy, one village-based, for local production and consumption, the other urban, cash-based, and oriented to commercial trade. Many of the French and Chinese took advantage of the differential between the two economies, gathering large profits to themselves at the expense of the rural peasants.

In contrast to the Buddhist countries of Cambodia and Laos, Vietnam has been influenced by China. This has separated them from their neighbors despite a common French occupation. The French entered Vietnam in 1777 to assist in suppressing a peasant uprising against the ruling Vietnamese families. The occasion provided France the opportunity to counter growing British and Dutch influence in Southeast Asia. The subsequent treaty of 1787 gave the French exclusive trading rights and access to ports. However, the terms of this treaty were never carried out due to the events of the French Revolution and Napoleonic Wars. Throughout the early 1800s, the

French attempt to renegotiate these trade terms met with little success. Their opportunity finally came as the result of antimissionary activity in the north.

Catholic missionaries had made significant numbers of conversions in the north. Fearful of the effects of a growing Catholic minority, the royal court at Hue passed edicts of death against the missionaries. In response, the French landed military troops and began the conquest of Indochina, a struggle that took longer than expected. The French did not enjoy complete control of the region until the 1890s. When they did gain control, Vietnam was broken into three administrative areas: Tonkin, Annam, and Cochinchina. Each was administered separately, with distinct institutional structures and policies. The Vietnamese were denied freedom of speech and participation in the political process.[31] They were prohibited from traveling outside their own provinces without special identity papers. On orders of the governor-general their property could be confiscated, and they were subject to indefinite detention and imprisonment without grounds.

There were almost continuous rebellions against French rule. Most were rurally based guerrilla resistance movements which were to provide models for the later Viet Minh. Probably the most significant was the founding of the Revolutionary Youth Movement in Canton in 1925 by Ho Chi Minh. This later evolved into a political alliance known as the Indochina Communist Party in 1929, from which the Vietnamese Communist Party split in 1930. The worldwide depression, the heavy demands of the French during World War I, and the decline of the price of rice contributed to a number of strikes and rebellions in 1930. The French ruthlessly repressed these, and most of the resistance leaders went underground.

During World War II, following the fall of Paris, there was joint administration of Indochina by the Vichy French government and the Japanese. For the most part the Japanese tolerated and cooperated with the French administration. The Vichy government established extensive sports and youth organizations in an attempt to retain the loyalty of the Vietnamese. This proved counterproductive, as these provided the Vietnamese resistance with models of organization and a means of heightening political awareness and discipline.

The Japanese took complete power in 1945. Their defeat created a power vacuum that was filled by Ho Chi Minh and his well-disciplined followers. They had been fighting in the northern mountains and so were able to step in and take control of Hanoi. They immediately initiated programs of government and land reform. The French, with British and U.S. support, reinvaded Indochina in an attempt to reassert their control. The First Indochina War was the result. Ho retreated to the countryside where he built a widely based guerrilla movement. By 1954 the Viet Minh and the North Vietnamese army controlled two-thirds of Vietnam. The French were defeated at Dien Bien Phu and the Geneva Conference was convened in an attempt to find a way to extricate France from its colonial morasse. Recognizing the power of Ho's forces, the country was divided into regroupment zones at the 17th parallel. This was not a political boundary or an attempt to divide the country.

Elections scheduled for 1956 were to provide for the reunification of Vietnam as an independent country. The United States, which by 1954 was underwriting 80 percent of the French war effort, strongly objected to the Geneva accords and refused to be a signatory. Realizing that in free elections Ho would certainly win, the United States gave its support to a little-known and unpopular Catholic from central Vietnam, Ngo Dinh Diem. Diem introduced a referendum in 1955 in which he proposed the creation of an independent republic of South Vietnam with himself as prime minister. In a highly questionable vote, Diem won 98.2 percent of the votes, including 605,025 votes from the 450,000 registered voters of Saigon.

The United States sent propaganda teams to the north prior to the division of the country to spread rumors of a bloodbath if the Catholics stayed. Nearly a million people left the north in 1954, two-thirds of them Catholics. Most of the Catholics were settled around Saigon, where they provided Diem with a strong political base. The influx of Catholic refugees tripled the total number of Catholics in South Vietnam. Diem also centralized his control of the government, appointing many members of his family to important government positions.

The U.S. reaction to the developments in South Vietnam included an average of $270 million a year in aid by 1956, and the provision of a Military Assistance Advisory Group (MAAG) of some eight hundred officers. The aid program was administered by a U.S. Operations Mission (USOM) under the advisement of a group of researchers from Michigan State University. Many of the Viet Minh cadres had remained in the south, and they continued to build a parallel administrative structure which was locally based and responsive to peasants' needs, in contrast to the often arrogant and repressive administration of the government in Saigon.

In 1956 Diem abolished the elected village councils, replacing them with officials directly appointed by the provincial governors. Another presidential order, issued the same year, gave the police wide powers of detainment of suspected Viet Minh or their sympathizers, powers which were often abused. In a 1959 attempt to deny the countryside to the Viet Minh, Diem initiated "agrovilles." These were enclosed and fortified villages in which the villagers were confined at night, surrounded by barbed wire and staked moats. Their fields were often located far from these villages. The government then proceeded to burn down the villagers' homes and to declare the zones outside the agrovilles free fire zones, in which anything moving after curfew would be shot. In most areas, about 70 percent of the villages were destroyed. After the villagers had been displaced, the United States would open the area to a variety of artillery and air attacks. Those who remained usually went underground, living in an extensive network of tunnels.

Although the fortified settlements went by different names, they most closely resembled concentration camps. By 1963, there were 8 million peasants living in these camps. Families were often forcibly relocated from militarily sensitive areas. Although the reason for such isolation and confinement was to deny the Viet Minh support, the effect was often the opposite. The Saigon government ruled with a shaky hand by day, but the night belonged to the Viet Minh. In the village of An Binh, in the Mekong Delta region, Sheehan reported that a government official slept in a different house each night to avoid assassination.[32] In many such "pacified" villages Americans and Vietnamese government officials were subject to assassination, so they traveled only in armed groups.

Diem finally proved too unpopular, and became more of a liability than an asset to the United States. A coup, at least tacitly supported by the United States, removed Diem and his brother from office in 1963. From 1963 to 1965 there were several changes in governments. Air Vice-Marshal Ky came to power in 1965. The same year the United States began a major escalation of the war, introducing ground troops and beginning intensive bombing of the countryside. The attempt to deny the Viet Cong the countryside resulted in its destruction. The Viet Cong, being mobile, could simply move on to other areas. The peasants who were tied to the land, on the other hand, lost nearly everything. Between 1965 and 1968, 3 million people were officially listed as refugees.[33] It was unofficially estimated that 2–3 million more were displaced persons.

The population of Saigon quintupled within a decade. The official refugee camps were squalid, often with no sanitary facilities. The daily official relief payment of 10 piasters (about eight cents U.S.) often never made it to the refugees, an estimated 75 percent of it being siphoned off by corrupt officials. In order to reduce the official numbers of refugees, the government would sometimes declare the camps to be permanent settlements. By 1969 South Vietnam had shifted from 85 percent rural to nearly 50 percent urban. The South Vietnamese government controlled the cities, and the Communists controlled the rural areas. Massive bombing and defoliation continued to devastate the countryside.

The United States sent hundreds of specialists, technicians, and researchers into Vietnam. Most worked under the auspices of AID. Few understood the problems of Vietnam, or acknowledged the role of the United States in the creation or aggravation of these problems.[34] The answer always seemed to be more aid, more goods, and more specialists. Much of the aid and goods disappeared into the labyrinthine maze of Vietnamese corruption. Furthermore, Vietnam's agriculture was almost completely destroyed, requiring the import of large quantities of rice. The biggest industry in Vietnam was the provision of services to the Americans stationed there. Productive capacity declined in the wake of the enormous import of American manufactured goods.

The United States seemed to believe that it was winning the war in 1967. The 1968 Tet offensive destroyed this belief, as the Viet Minh and North Vietnamese army attempted to gain control of the southern cities. The United States was often forced to destroy up to 50 percent of these cities in order to retake them. This, and growing domestic pressure to pull out of an unpopular and confusing war, led the United States to begin looking for a negotiated settlement. In 1973 the Paris peace talks concluded with the United States setting a timetable for complete withdrawal of its troops and the turning of the war effort over to the Army of the Republic of Vietnam (ARVN). At the same time, Congress approved massive aid cuts to South Vietnam. The consequences of the U.S. withdrawal and aid cutbacks were devastating to the South Vietnamese economy. By 1975, there were 3.5 million unemployed in South Vietnam, agriculture was at a standstill, industrial capacity was 60 percent, inflation was 114 percent, and devaluation of the piaster had resulted in price increases of 50–300 percent. The ARVN was short on supplies, fuel, spare parts, and ammunition.

The North Vietnamese began a conventional invasion of the south following the U.S. withdrawal and made significant gains. The end for the south came rapidly and with it the desperate last minute flight from an expected bloodbath in Saigon, an expectation that had been promoted by United States and Vietnamese government spokesmen.

The bloodbath did not materialize. However, economic conditions in the south remain very poor, with corruption still a major problem. The attempt by the north to assert its control was hampered by the longstanding cultural differences between the north and south, as well as the effects of the American presence. Austerity measures have been badly received by the Saigonese in particular. The presence of the Vietnamese in Cambodia has also necessitated an apparently permanent mobilization of the population.

Russian aid for Vietnam is estimated to be $8 million per day.[35] The destruction of the countryside poses enormous problems for agricultural development. The new government introduced New Economic Zones in 1976, which were often inhospitable and plagued by a lack of tools, fertilizer, and other necessities. In 1977 the government began to forcibly relocate people to these zones. In addition, bad weather and poor harvests have contributed to malnutrition. Unemployment remains high, and industry is operating at far less than capacity.

Ethnic Chinese in Vietnam

The history of Chinese immigration into Indochina extends over two thousand years. Many came by sea, settling in Cochinchina and Cambodia. Others came overland to Tonkin and Annam. With few exceptions they retained their own set of institutions, refusing to be assimilated into the larger population. This maintenance of close ties with China and retention of a strong separate ethnic identity has caused tensions between the Chinese and their host populations. In addition, by virtue of their enterprise and role as "strangers" they have come to occupy positions of wealth as middlemen and money lenders.[36] They also dominate the highly skilled cultivation of peppers, and enjoy a near monopoly on the milling of rice.

The Chinese in Southeast Asia are five-sixths of the total overseas Chinese population.[37] Of these, by far the highest concentration has been in Vietnam. The highly sinicized nature of Vietnamese society and long history of contact with China would seem to suggest positive relations between the Vietnamese and ethnic Chinese. This has not been the case. The Chinese in Vietnam have been subject to numerous repressive measures designed to break their economic control over trade and retail activities.

French attempts to discourage Chinese immigration and competition with French commercial interests resulted in the decrees of 1874 and 1876 and the formation of an immigration service. In addition, the French levied a heavy poll tax and a special personal capital tax proportionate to profits made. Chinese competition with the French was aided by the resident Chinese familiarity with local culture and an extensive network of contacts and associations. Accounts were kept in Chinese, a language the French could not read. Chinese ownership of junks and sampans meant control of the transport of goods, particularly rice. They also enjoyed a nearly exclusive position as brokers for the export of rice.[38] This economic control has been a continuing source of resentment and justification for attempts to forcibly integrate the Chinese, by both Vietnamese and French governments.

The Chinese formed their own enclaves, called *bangs* (congregations). Local authorities appointed community leaders for these groups who were responsible for the behavior of the community and the payment of taxes. In the south, these community leaders, appointed by the French, enjoyed considerable police and fiscal power. This led to Chinese protests in 1930, 1935, and 1946. The last of these protests ended with the French granting veto power over candidates to the local Chinese consul. The Chinese also maintained their own separate Chinese language schools and newspapers.

Following the partition of 1954, the South Vietnamese implemented a policy of forced integration. In 1956 they declared that all

Chinese born in Vietnam were to be considered Vietnamese. Non-Vietnamese were excluded from eleven occupations, including most retail occupations and the middleman trade in rice. This resulted in many Chinese business closings and withdrawals of bank funds. The severe economic problems that this created for the Vietnamese forced a relaxation of the policy.[39] In the north, the process of assimilation was eased by the fact that many of the Chinese were industrial workers or fishermen. Also, the socialization of the economic system eliminated private trade. The North Vietnamese government naturalized all the resident Chinese in 1961.

Following reunification in 1975, the new government was faced with the problem of integrating the large Chinese population of the south. This was complicated by a growing nationalist feeling among the Chinese and the liberalized policies of the new leadership in China. In January 1976 the ethnic Chinese in Vietnam were required to register their citizenship. Although the results of this effort were never released, it seems that the number who registered as Chinese far exceeded the number who registered as Vietnamese.

Another order to register was given in February 1976. Those who retained Chinese citizenship were subjected to heavy taxes, occupational discrimination, and reduction of their food ration. In September 1976 all Chinese schools and newspapers were closed. By 1977 the border dispute with Cambodia intensified. China supported Cambodia, and made threatening noises regarding its own border with Vietnam. In February 1977 those who had registered as Chinese were summarily dismissed from their jobs, their residence registration canceled, and their food rations stopped; they were prohibited from civil service or public enterprises, retail trades, and farming. They were also forbidden to move from place to place. Many were expelled, under the guise of "voluntary repatriation," and their property seized.

By the end of July 1978 more than 160,000 ethnic Chinese had fled into China. Many more left the south by boat. Eighty-five percent of the boat people in 1978 were ethnic Chinese, and over a two-year period they accounted for 70 percent of the total number of boat people refugees. By 1980, 400,000 ethnic Chinese had fled by boat. It is estimated that, if as many as half of the boat people refugees died in transit, and if 200,000 fled overland to China, the ethnic Chinese population in Vietnam is now practically nonexistent. In addition, by charging high prices to allow the Chinese to leave, Vietnam has taken in enormous sums of money, making its refugee trade the number one source of foreign revenue. In the month of April 1979, a total of US$242 million were sent by overseas Chinese to enable friends and relatives to buy their way out of Vietnam. Vietnam is estimated to have made up to US$3 billion in the refugee trade during that year.

Conclusion

The prearrival experiences of Indochinese refugees are unlike those of most immigrants to America. Their experiences range from those of the urbanized Vietnamese to those of the rural tribesmen of Laos. Many of these refugees have experienced previous displacement in movements for political independence. The Vietnam War only added to a long tradition of movement and adaptation to new environments. However, forced migration on such a massive scale was not experienced in the area before the fall of South Vietnam.

In the nine years since the 1975 collapse of Saigon, the United States has been involved in the resettlement of more than 670,000 Indochinese refugees. Other countries participating in this resettlement effort have accepted more than 345,000 additional Indochinese refugees, with France, Canada, Australia, and West Germany taking the largest numbers. Such large numbers require a comprehensive set of public policies to direct and aid resettlement. In the following chapters we explore the federal policy of resettlement in the United States and the subnational policies of local governments. Within this matrix of intergovernmental politics we find the problems and potentials associated with this forced migration.

3
Federal Resettlement Policy

The U.S. government, surprised by the suddenness of the collapse of the South Vietnamese government, worked through March and April of 1975 to develop plans for the evacuation of American dependents and Indochinese who had supported U.S. policy. In hearings of the U.S. Senate Judiciary Committee's Subcommittee on Refugees and Escapees, the American commitment was noted as originally limited to the evacuation of American dependents and current employees of the U.S. government, approximately 17,600 people. The inclusion of all former employees of the United States and persons whose lives the government thought were endangered was not made until just before the 30 April fall of Saigon.[1]

By 28 April, the categories that had been targeted for evacuation and "parole" included 4,000 orphans, 10,000 to 75,000 relatives of American citizens or permanent resident aliens, and 50,000 "high-risk" Vietnamese, including past and present government employees, officials who cooperated in the evacuation, those with knowledge of U.S. government intelligence operations, vulnerable political or intellectual figures, Communist defectors, employees of U.S. firms, and participants in U.S. government–sponsored programs. However, it soon became clear than many of those who had already left Indochina were not those whom the U.S. government had intended to evacuate. The Immigration and Naturalization Service informed the Senate Judiciary Committee that a new category had been established as a "catchall" to accommodate refugees who had fled spontaneously and did not meet the original criteria established for parole.

On 18 April 1975, President Ford had authorized the parole of 130,000 Indochinese refugees into the United States and assigned responsibility for managing and coordinating the effort to the Interagency Task Force for Indochinese Refugees (IATF). The IATF was composed of eighteen federal departments and agencies, each with its own expertise and abilities to aid in the evacuation and resettlement. A few days earlier, the U.S. mission at Geneva requested assistance from the United Nations High Commissioner for Refugees (UNHCR) and the Intergovernmental Committee for European Migration (ICEM) in locating third countries willing to accept refugees from Indochina.

On 22 April 1975, the IATF asked civil and military authorities on Guam to prepare to provide ninety days of care and maintenance for 50,000 refugees being evacuated from South Vietnam. When the IATF's advance party arrived on Guam, on 25 April, there were already 10,000 refugees on the island who had arrived by military and commercial aircraft. By the 28th, one day prior to the final evacuation of Saigon, there were more than 20,000 arrivals, and by 14 May 1975, there were more than 50,000 arrivals. Additional refugees were also arriving in the Phillipines, Wake Island, Thailand, and Hawaii.

As the number of refugees continued to mount in the Pacific sites, the IATF began to open Reception Centers on the U.S. mainland. Camp Pendleton, California; Fort Indiantown Gap, Pennsylvania; Eglin Air Force Base, Florida; and Fort Chaffee, Arkansas, were designated Reception Centers to house and process Indochinese refugees. The major purpose of the centers, besides the task of Immigration and Naturalization Service clearance, was to reduce the possibility of the refugees becoming public charges. The centers were transitional institutions where refugees were processed into immigrants and oriented to American life. The average stay in the centers was seven months. "Transition America" was the official cultural orientation program implemented at the centers. American movies were shown, and classes on employment and English were conducted.

Of this first wave of 130,000 Indochinese refugees, 8,182 had at least $4,000 and were released into the United States following security checks. The remaining 121,610 found sponsors through the efforts of voluntary agencies.[2] All first wave refugees were released from the Reception Centers by December 1975.

This chapter describes the resettlement process that began with these events and the legislation that has governed it. The chapter is divided into four sections. The first describes the circumstances surrounding the 1978 resurgence of the exodus from Indochina and the U.S. response to this resurgence. The second section describes the evolution of U.S. refugee legislation. The third describes the resettlement role of the voluntary agencies. And the fourth describes the impact that refugee resettlement has had on local areas.

The Second Wave

Natural disasters and new political upheavals precipitated a second and more massive exodus of Indochinese refugees starting in late 1978. In Cambodia, Hanoi overthrew the government of Pol Pot, causing over 100,000 Cambodians to seek asylum in Thailand. A number of the early arrivals in this second wave were educated and from urban areas. They, along with a much larger number of starving Cambodian peasants, congregated along the Thai-Cambodian border and in camps set up for Cambodians by the Thai government. By 1980 a continuing Cambodian famine had forced over 150,000 people into the Thai facilities.

At the same time, 85,000 refugees left Vietnam in small craft never intended for open seas. The exodus was triggered by bad weather, a deteriorating economy, and pressure brought about by the conflict with Cambodia. Sixty percent of the boat people were ethnic Chinese caught in a renewal of racial hatred that was exacerbated by a Chinese border excursion. Hanoi had also found it difficult to compete with the private sector in the south. They viewed the Chinese, many of whom were members of the merchant class, as "bourgeois" elements and encouraged their departure, often accepting bribes to look the other way. Others in the business and professional classes left when all trading and business operations were abolished and currency reforms were instituted. This exodus became a deluge in 1979, when over 56,000 Vietnamese left in the month of June alone.[3]

While world attention was focused on the dramatic escape of the boat people, the numbers of refugees crossing the Mekong River into Thailand from Laos began to increase. The Pathet Lao campaign to punish the Hmong and drive them out of their highland homes has already been described. In addition, the Laotian government attempted to establish new economic policies, nationalizing the retail trade as had been done in Vietnam. The merchant and professional classes, who were largely ethnic Chinese, began to seek asylum in Thailand. Other groups of Laotians also began to appear in the Thai camps. These had been recently released from the harsh "seminars" that had been organized by the Pathet Lao to re-educate those who had shared power prior to the Communist takeover in 1975.[4]

As the number of Laotian refugees entering Thailand continued to climb, the Thai government began to reconsider its view on their motivation. Perhaps it was not persecution, but the fact that life in the refugee camps was superior to the hardships of life at home, that led these people to migrate. On 1 January 1981, the Thai government instituted a program of "humane deterrence," in which new arrivals would not be eligible for third country repatriation. This policy reduced the Laotian outflow from more than 3,000 per month to fewer than 1,000 per month.[5]

The occupational profile of Indochinese refugees changed during the second wave. The second wave contained a larger percentage of farmers and fishermen. Second wave refugees also tended to be younger than first wave refugees. While first wave refugees were primarily Vietnamese, the second wave contained large numbers of Khmer, Lao, and ethnic Chinese. The second wave refugees have also been less well-educated than the first wave, many coming from nonliterate or only marginally literate societies.[6]

These events, combined with increasing hostilities toward refugees in countries of first asylum, led to a renewed U.S. interest in the Indochinese refugee situation. In 1978 Congress authorized the admission by parole of 53,000 additional Indochinese refugees. It also committed itself to admitting an additional 25,000 a year over the next few years.[7]

When Malaysia, Hong Kong, and Singapore began to turn boats away, a 1979 Geneva convention was organized to deal with the refugee problem on a worldwide basis. By then, there were over 225,000 Indochinese refugees in the first asylum camps. At Geneva, the first asylum countries agreed to permit the refugees to enter their camps if acceptance was linked to expeditious resettlement to third countries. In response to this situation, President Carter decided to increase the number of refugees who could be accepted by the United States. After a 1979 consultation with Congress, refugee flow was targeted at 84,000 a year. However, by June the situation had worsened and the president announced his intention to double the monthly refugee acceptance rate to 14,000. Sponsorship efforts were itensified, and by September 1979 more than 14,000 refugees were being resettled in the United States.

Initial resettlement in the United States was directed toward "boat cases" since these refugees were not welcome in the first asylum camps in Malaysia due to racial conflict. The United States did not begin to admit larger numbers of Laotians and Cambodians until their numbers defied accommodation in the Thai camps.

Federal Refugee Legislation

The original "parole" of 130,000 people was carried out under provisions of the Immigration and Nationality Act of 1952, which authorizes the granting of the tentative status of "parole" by the attorney general. In 1976–77, a series of additional paroles were initiated to admit Laotians who had not been included in the parole program in April 1975, as well as other Indochinese refugees who had not been evacuated during the chaos and who were now stranded in Thai camps. The Thai government had been assured that this latter group would be removed and resettled elsewhere.

The Indochina Migration and Refugee Assistance Act of 1975 allocated funds for the movement and resettlement of Vietnamese, Cambodian, and Laotian refugees. Government officials estimated that a two-year period would be sufficient for the assimilation of these refugees into American society, and so authorized the act to expire 30 September 1977. Assistance to Indochinese refugees was provided on the same basis as Aid to Families with Dependent Children (AFDC), except that the requirements relating to family composition were waived. Because of the large average size of Indochinese refugee households and the low average wages received by the wage earners, the government allowed families with heads of households to continue to receive AFDC benefits.

For low-income refugees who were incapable of self-support because of old age, blindness, or other disabilities, the government provided Supplemental Security Income (SSI). Needy refugees who were not eligible for either SSI or AFDC could receive Refugee Cash

Assistance or Refugee Medical Assistance, which provided full federal reimbursements based on the same income limitations and payment levels as applied in a state's AFDC program.

Support services for Indochinese refugees were 100 percent federally funded under the Indochinese Refugee Assistance Program (IRAP). IRAP funds were distributed through two channels: Title XX programs that were already being provided to other state residents, and Special Projects that were directly funded by the Department of Health and Human Services (formerly HEW). The special projects have focused on the provision of technical assistance, information concerning English as a Second Language (ESL) instruction, Indochinese languages and cross-cultural differences, and techniques for language training.

Due to the ad hoc nature of the parole authorities and the absence of overall planning and coordination, refugees initially received varying degrees of support and assistance, depending on the state in which they were resettled. While the average per capita cash assistance payment was $305 in 1977, Mississippi provided $21 and California provided $489. While the average per capita medical assistance payment was $155, Mississippi provided $13 and California provided $235.[8]

The Indochinese Migration and Refugee Assistance Act expired on 30 September 1977, and funds for FY78 were not approved until 7 March 1978. This delay created numerous difficulties and uncertainties for states. Many could not meet refugee needs until new appropriations were made in March 1978. Eleven states suspended their IRAP programs during this period, and Missouri refused to reinstate its refugee program after the March appropriation.

Since the beginning of IRAP in 1975, states have been required to provide the same social services to refugees as to nonrefugees. However, states were reimbursed by IRAP for all funds spent for Indochinese refugees under Title XX programs. In 1979, states were allowed to provide additional federally funded services, such as assessment and manpower employment services, ESL, vocational training, skills recertification, day care, and transportation when the services were determined to be related to employment. This action was taken to assist states in acquiring the services needed to help refugees become self-sufficient. Many states could not afford to develop these services independently. Indeed, to avoid the burden of an increased service bureaucracy, some states subcontracted with private service providers for the provision of these newly funded services.

In February 1979, the Office of Coordinator of Refugee Affairs was established to provide permanent guidelines for refugee admissions. In March 1980, the Refugee Act gave the office its mandate to coordinate domestic and international resettlement programs, design an overall budget strategy for presentation to Congress, advise the president and federal agencies on policy, represent the United States with foreign governments, and develop liaisons between elements in government and all others involved in refugee resettlement. The act replaced existing ad hoc, nationality-specific programs with a single, permanent Refugee Resettlement Program (RRP). It defined a refugee as a person outside his or her country of nationality who is unable or unwilling to return to that country because of persecution or a well-founded fear of persecution on account of race, religion, nationality, membership in a particular social group, or political opinion.

The act created the Office of Refugee Resettlement (ORR) within the Department of Health and Human Services to oversee state-administered delivery systems for refugee cash assistance, medical assistance, and social services. In 1981, ORR moved to a system of state-administered refugee resettlement programs. The states were required to submit plans to ORR for services they would provide and to appoint a state coordinator to be responsible for overseeing each state's plan.

The Refugee Act of 1980 authorized ORR to continue to reimburse states for up to 100 percent of their costs in providing cash and medical assistance to eligible refugees. But, for the first time, it established a time limitation on reimbursements to states. The federal government felt that, without a time limit on federally funded support, refugees would develop a welfare mentality and states would not feel the necessity of helping refugees become self-sufficient. As of April 1981, federal reimbursement funding was to be provided only during the first thirty-six months that the refugee was in the United States.

As economic conditions continued to deteriorate and the welfare dependency rate climbed, refugees were increasingly viewed as expecting support for three years while receiving educational assistance. In March 1982, new federal regulations reduced refugee eligibility limits to eighteen months and eliminated the $30 and one-third income disregard that had been given to refugees under AFDC. This disregard allowed refugees to deduct the first $30 of their income and one-third of any additional income before their AFDC eligibility was determined. Social service funding continued to focus on employment-related services, English language training, and case management services. Local resettlement agencies and state and local governments were instructed to coordinate their efforts in these areas.

Other provisions of the Refugee Assistance Amendments of 1982 required refugees to register for employment services within the first sixty days of arrival, participate in job and language training as a condition of receiving cash assistance, and to notify sponsors or voluntary agencies when applying for public assistance. These provisions also made full-time students ineligible for cash assistance.

Voluntary Agencies and Sponsorship

Although the IATF and ORR have been responsible for allocating refugee funds, for evacuating refugees, and for organizing resettlement strategies, they have delegated the responsibility for initial resettlement of refugees to a small number of private, nonprofit voluntary resettlement agencies. Voluntary agencies have been involved in the resettlement of refugees since World War II, when they provided resettlement assistance without government financial support. In the case of Indochinese refugees, the Indochinese Refugee Assistance Program provides contractual funding to the voluntary agencies for the resettlement of these refugees.

The Department of State accredits voluntary agencies based on the criteria of well-established national networks, ability to raise private funds, and willingness to resettle refugees from any country of origin. Under broadly defined contracts, voluntary agencies were initially given grants of $500 for each refugee resettled. Those involved with the initial resettlement of Indochinese refugees include the United States Catholic Conference (USCC), American Fund for Czechoslovak Refugees (AFCR), Church World Services (CWS), Lutheran Immigration and Refugee Services (LIRS), United Hebrew Immigration and Assistance Service (United HIAS), International Rescue Committee (IRC), American Council of Nationality Services (ACNS), Traveler's Aid International Social Services, and the Tolstoy Foundation.

The procedure for voluntary agency intervention in the resettlement process is as follows. First, the U.S. embassy and INS review the cases of refugees who are residing in first asylum camps. If these refugees are approved for resettlement in the United States, their files are sent to the American Council of Voluntary Agencies (ACVA), in New York, which serves as a clearinghouse for voluntary agencies. Refugees without sponsors are divided among ACVA members according to their capacity to provide needed services. When the ACVA has secured voluntary agency sponsorships, it sends its assurances to representatives in Southeast Asia.

The voluntary agencies and the Intergovernmental Committee for Migration, formerly ICEM, are responsible for the processing of refugees out of the first asylum countries. The voluntary agencies handle legal documentation and airport reception. When a refugee arrives at the final destination, the local voluntary agency office counsels the refugee regarding health, employment, social, and vocational services. The voluntary agency may provide funding and in-kind donations to sponsors. Sponsors provide the initial resettlement needs for food, clothing, and housing. When the sponsor is unwilling or unable to meet the total needs of the refugee, or when the refugee terminates the sponsorship, the refugee registers for county social services and becomes dependent upon public assistance until self-reliance can be achieved.

Obviously, sponsorship is the essential element of voluntary agency activity. Each refugee or refugee family is required to have a local sponsor, identified by a voluntary agency, who is willing to assume responsibility for providing the essential support necessary for integration into the American economy and society. These sponsors, in conjunction with the voluntary agencies, are expected to provide food, clothing, and shelter; assistance in finding employment; help with school enrollment; and coverage of ordinary medical costs until the refugee becomes self-sufficient. The moral obligation to provide this support contributed to an initially wide dispersion of the refugee population since, within a given community, few individuals could afford to provide sponsorship and few groups were available to do so.[9]

Initially, refugees were given an option as to which voluntary agency would find them a sponsor. However, as speed of resettlement became the priority the IATF began to assign refugees to voluntary agencies. The resettlement effort was taking place at a time when economic conditions in the United States were deteriorating. Unemployment had reached 8.9 percent and a Gallup poll indicated that a majority of Americans were opposed to the admission of the refugees.[10] The IATF set as its policy a rapid and wide dispersion of refugees to minimize the economic impact and political unrest that might be caused by heavy concentrations of refugees in areas that already suffered from high unemployment and limited housing. To further speed up the process, the IATF gave the voluntary agencies forty-five days to locate a sponsor and complete the processing. If they failed, the refugee was reassigned to another agency.[11]

The speed with which the voluntary agencies were expected to process refugees made it impossible for them to investigate sponsorship situations. This led to a number of cases of refugee exploitation and employment below the minimum wage.[12] The IATF policy of wide dispersion also created problems. Voluntary agencies often split extended families into several households and resettled them in different areas. This frequently led to relocations (secondary migration) soon after refugees left the processing centers.[13]

Of the $58 million in resettlement fees that had originally been committed to the voluntary agencies for first wave resettlement, only $36 million had been spent by December 1975 when the last of the first wave refugees had been relocated. In a Report to the Congress, the Comptroller General questioned the legitimacy of the payment of the last $22 million and criticized the vagueness of the contract arrangements between the voluntary agencies and the State Department. It also called for an audit and investigation to determine how money was to be spent after December 1975.[14] In order to avoid some of the problems associated with the contracts, the report recommended that a definition of the term *resettlement* be included in future contracts. It was also recommended that unused funds be returned to the State Department after the 1977 completion of the program, that a specific fee, less than $500, be paid to the voluntary agencies for resettlement of refugees who had their own sponsors, and that reporting procedures be improved to permit monitoring of the program's progress and to provide data on family status, language ability, employment, health, housing, public assistance, and sponsor relationship status. As of June 1976, the government had received only 42,000 progress reports on the 116,000 refugees who were processed by the five major voluntary agencies.

Affected Communities

Two developments in the resettlement of Indochinese refugees have created serious problems for the state, county, and local governments that must implement the assistance component of federal resettlement policy. First, despite a stated policy of dispersion, refugees have tended to cluster, through secondary migration, in a relatively few locations. The distribution of the refugee population, given in appendix A by year, state, and ethnicity, reveals the effect of this clustering. California, for example, is home for about one-third of the total refugee population. Continuing clustering is predictable, given the importance of the role of the family to these refugees and the fact that voluntary agencies have better-developed infrastructures for receiving refugees in areas where refugee populations are already large. However, the clustering does burden the service delivery mechanisms of the affected areas.

Second, under new resettlement legislation, these areas are likely to include a large number of refugees who require assistance but who do not qualify for federal reimbursement of assistance expenses. In June 1983 the National Association of Counties recommended that the provisions of the Refugee Act be strengthened to require the involvement of local officials and federal reimbursement for medical and cash payments to "time expired" refugees who are not self-sufficient.[15] This group felt that federal policy was responsible for the presence of these refugees in their communities and that the federal government should pay for its policy. Therefore, it recommended that cash assistance and medical assistance last at least thirty-six months.

Many areas in California have been overwhelmed by the influx of the secondary migrants. In Contra Costa County, California, 40 percent of the 3,000 refugees receiving public assistance are secondary migrants, and 20 percent of these are time expired. In Los Angeles County, nearly 50,000 refugees are receiving cash assistance, 30 percent of whom are secondary migrants. Between October 1981 and December 1982, Alameda County experienced a 44 percent increase in its refugee caseload. In October 1979 Fresno County had 400 refugees receiving public assistance. Three years later, 5,400 cases were on public assistance. In Stanislaus County, 71 percent of its 3,000 refugees are secondary migrants and 84 percent of these are Aid to Families with Dependent Children (AFDC) and Refugee Cash Assistance (RCA) recipients who will soon become "time expired" and require county funding for services.[16]

Counties in Minnesota are experiencing similar problems. Ramsey County, Minnesota, has approximately 9,000 refugees, 80 percent of whom are Hmong. The secondary migration rate in the county is 40 percent, and only 28 percent of the refugee population qualifies for public assistance within the time limitation set by the federal government.[17] In St. Paul, 11 percent of the school population is Indochinese; over $840,000 in local property taxes and $750,000 in state and federal monies have been spent on programs to aid the Indochinese school population.[18]

The Office of Refugee Resettlement has offered grant money to affected counties under its Refugee Targeted Assistance Program (RTAP) to support projects designed to improve economic self-sufficiency and reduce dependency. ORR is encouraging innovative approaches by local governments. Funds may not be used for duplicating existing service delivery systems or for venture capital either as grants or loans. Targeted Assistance Grants are used to solicit greater private sector involvement and to operate job-training programs. The Targeted Assistance approach focuses on the use of participants' native skills and abilities to find employment, and it is directed toward refugees who are receiving public assistance.

Conclusion

The resettlement of Indochinese refugees has resulted in the development of cooperation between public and private authorities. While the voluntary agencies have been delegated the responsibility of initial resettlement, the federal government has assumed much of the burden for the financing and processing of refugees for resettlement.

Clearly, the resettlement of such a large group of refugees in such a short period of time poses some obvious conflicts between the federal and subnational governments. Yet subnational governments have adopted and created a variety of programs designed to ease the burden of resettlement for themselves and the refugees they serve. The following chapter describes the uncertainties and problems that these governments have faced, as well as the resettlement policies they have developed.

4
Subnational Resettlement Policies

As indicated in the previous chapter, states were initially given the responsibility for administering refugee cash assistance and medical assistance programs, and for providing social services that were mandated under their Title XX social service plans. These services were sometimes provided directly by states, sometimes contracted out to private service providers, and sometimes provided through a mix of both approaches. In any case, the services were mandated by the federal government.

The Refugee Act of 1980 assigned the states a larger role in the development, implementation, and administration of refugee programs. Each state is now required to file a State Refugee Resettlement Plan and to appoint a Refugee Coordinator for coordinating publicly and privately funded resettlement programs. In addition, states have assumed full responsibility for planning and managing refugee cash assistance, medical assistance, and social service programs.

Subnational Effects

The several changes in federal funding that have occurred since 1980 have had major effects on state approaches to refugee service provision. The thirty-six-month and eighteen-month eligibility restrictions, and elimination of the $30 and one-third income disregard are prime examples. Time-expired refugees continue to be eligible for existing aid programs if they meet regular eligibility standards, but all of these programs are funded under normal federal/state/county sharing ratios and are not 100 percent federally reimbursed.

The impact of the eighteen-month eligibility restriction has been most strongly felt by selected county governments and needy refugees. As needy refugees reach time-expired status, they will either enroll in existing county-funded General Assistance programs or move to counties that provide these programs. Oregon, which has no General Assistance program, reported an estimated 15 percent of its total refugee population moved in anticipation of the changes in federal funding, most of them to California. In Washington, nearly 40 percent of the time-expired refugees moved between February and August 1982. Fourteen percent moved out of state, with the majority moving to California. This response to the changes in federal reimbursement policy has led many states to revise their refugee resettlement programs, reducing the social service emphasis and increasing the emphasis on employment-related services.

Additional reductions in the federal social service budget have resulted in a continued decline in federal refugee funding levels. California, with the largest number of refugees, has been hardest hit by these reductions. Its 1982 expenses are not fully covered by federal funds, leaving it with an estimated shortfall of between $57 million and $67 million. This shortfall situation is expected to continue, as ORR requests for FY84 are $97.2 million less than FY83 appropriations.

Secondary migration has been a major factor in the inequity of the burden faced by those counties and cities with large refugee populations. Although the original resettlement plan did call for a dispersion of refugees in an attempt to lessen their visibility and impact, its failure soon became evident. Refugees moved for a variety of reasons. There were problems with sponsors who did not fully realize the implications of caring for a family that came from a very different cultural setting. Family reunification of extended families, already existing Asian communities, climate, employment possibilities, and the extent of funding for welfare services were also major considerations in moving.

Since 1976 refugees have moved to urban areas in California, Texas, and Louisiana; they have left Kansas, Kentucky, New Mexico, North Dakota, and Oklahoma. For example, in January 1976, California had 21.6 percent of the Indochinese refugee population. In January 1977 the California population was 24.4 percent. Between

February 1978 and February 1979, California received 70.9 percent of the secondary migration of Indochinese refugees, increasing California's share of the refugee population to 31 percent.

Increased refugee concentrations resulting from secondary migration imposed disproportionate burdens on selected states. In response, new strategies were developed to alter refugee migration patterns. For example, a Khmer-guided placement project was instituted in 1979 in an attempt to reduce the flow of Cambodian refugees to Long Beach, California. The project placed about 8,500 Cambodian "free cases"—those who did not have any close relatives already in the United States—in twelve sites, in numbers ranging from 300 to 1,300 at each site. Locations were selected on the basis of employment availability and housing, social service availability, and the presence of mutual assistance associations composed of Cambodians who could assist the new arrivals in becoming self-sufficient. In 1981 Georgia and Massachusetts had enough Cambodian refugees to be among the top ten states in Cambodian population.[1] Table 4.1 lists several states and their Indochinese populations.

In FY82, the ORR announced a placement policy designed to change the current geographic distribution. In order to avoid any additional impact on areas already experiencing heavy influx, voluntary agencies were instructed to attempt to place "free cases" in areas not already affected. In response to secondary migration, ORR is currently developing Favorable Alternative Sites Projects to locate communities that do not already have sizeable refugee populations and are willing to receive refugees. These sites are provided with additional funding for social services to develop ESL and employment services for refugees.[2]

Targeted assistance grants have also been developed in response to the burdens that have been placed on seriously affected counties. These grants provide local governments additional funds for employment services development.

Overview of Subnational Policies

A survey by Berkeley Planning Associates (BPA) of the administration of state resettlement programs in nine states found wide variations among these states in the structure of their programs. There are several reasons for this variation. Some states have been involved in

Table 4.1   Indochinese populations in selected states, 1982

State	Number
California	225,500
Texas	50,700
Washington	29,900
Pennsylvania	23,200
Illinois	21,700
Minnesota	21,200
Virginia	19,600
New York	18,300
Oregon	17,800
Louisiana	15,100
Massachusetts	12,000
Colorado	10,500
Florida	10,400
Michigan	9,500
Total	485,400
Other	134,400
Total	619,800

resettlement since 1975 while others were not actively involved before 1980. States also have divergent philosophies regarding their role in providing refugee social services. The size and visibility of refugee populations is also a major factor due to its effect on the level of competition between refugees and other state residents in need. In some states, resettlement is a highly visible and politically sensitive issue. In others, resettlement is a minor issue with low priority.

The majority of states have a single state agency which administers welfare and social services and which has been designated as the agency responsible for refugee resettlement. The state Refugee Coordinator may be the director of the single state agency (as in California and Pennsylvania), the assistant director (Texas), or be located within a subunit of that agency and report to the agency director through at least one intermediate level (Illinois).[3] There is also variation in the placement of the refugee program office within the single state agency. The BPA study found that, of the nine states studied, the placement of the refugee program office and its ability to influence the policy making were not closely linked. The size and visibility of the program, its level of political support, and the interest of the director in refugee issues were the more important factors.

Prior to 1980, most states used mainstream offices to provide refugee assistance. The Refugee Act of 1980 has had little effect on this. Wherever possible, state agencies have continued to rely upon mainstream offices and existing programs within state welfare and social service agencies for basic management functions. The development of policy guidelines, their implementation, and the supervision of the delivery of refugee cash and medical assistance programs is usually accomplished through these agencies.

California and Texas are the only states where these functions are located within the refugee program office. In other states, refugees have been mainstreamed through existing cash assistance programs for other state residents. Unfortunately, few of these cash assistance workers are bilingual or trained to deal with the problems of Indochinese refugee resettlement. However, in the case of Title XX services, even these states have tended to contract out to a mix of public and private service providers for employment programs specifically targeted to refugee assistance.

Recent budget cuts and relatively high dependency rates among refugees have contributed to the reduction in the diversity of programs offered by different states. Social services have been significantly reduced and preliterate and survival ESL and employment services have been given top priority in an attempt to foster refugee self-sufficiency in the shortest possible time. States have required all employable refugees receiving cash assistance to register with state or other employment service providers.

The continued emphasis on ESL as well as its high funding levels indicate a belief that some English language skills are essential to employment. The recent shift to survival ESL from general ESL classes has resulted in a redesign of some programs and a standardization of guidelines and program objectives for others. Service providers are developing competency-based curricula and imposing limits on the amount of time a refugee can spend in ESL classes.

ESL services are provided by a variety of contractors, with some states using mainstream educational institutions and other states using private service providers. California, Pennsylvania, Texas, and Minnesota use a mix of mainstream institutions and private service providers.

Reductions in attempts to deliver a comprehensive range of services to refugees are exemplified in the case of Pennsylvania. Until recently, it provided the widest range of services among the states. In FY82, its budget allocation for support services constituted 47 percent of the total social service allocation. In 1983, this figure was reduced to 6 percent. Permissible support services were limited to case management and emergency translation and interpretation.

Health services are primarily funded by three major sources. The federal government's Center for Disease Control (CDC) in Atlanta administers ORR funds that are granted to public health departments in high-impact refugee areas. These funds are now used for health assessment and follow-up of infectious diseases for initial placement and secondary migration refugees. States also use their own refugee social service allocations to fund health-related activities such as translation/interpretation, health information, and referral. Refugee Medical Assistance (RMA) funds may be used to reimburse refugee health service providers as long as the medical services provided are available to any other indigent state resident. These funds have been used by Washington and Utah to reimburse local health departments for refugee health services. Most other states have relied mainly on CDC funds for health screening and follow-up. In any case, the voluntary agency sponsors are usually responsible for ensuring that refugees obtain a health assessment.

The following sections describe the refugee resettlement programs of six states with large Indochinese refugee populations: California, Texas, Washington, Illinois, Pennsylvania, and Minnesota. Particular emphasis is given to California, as this state is the most seriously affected by a large refugee population and the site of our survey of refugee households.

California

California has been involved in refugee resettlement since April 1975, when the first refugee reception center opened at Camp Pendleton. It presently has the largest population of Indochinese refugees in the United States. As of September 1984 the estimated number of Indochinese refugees in the state was 259,100. Eighty-five percent of these are Vietnamese. Nearly 50 percent are concentrated in Los Angeles and Orange Counties. The city of Santa Ana, in Orange County, has the highest refugee ratio of any city in the United

States—1 out of every 12 residents. Merced County and Fresno County, both located in the heart of the San Joaquin Valley agricultural area, have recently seen a remarkable increase in the number of refugees, largely as a result of secondary migration. Many of the new arrivals are Hmong who are attracted by the rural setting and the opportunities for agricultural employment. From 1979 to 1982, Fresno County experienced a 1346 percent increase in the number of refugees on public assistance, from 400 in 1979 to 5,400 in 1982. Ninety-three percent were secondary migrants. Merced County has had an even greater increase, from 200 in 1980 to 6,000 in 1982.[4] This influx places a considerable burden on the local communities and on the resources of county-funded welfare programs.

The California refugee program is located within the umbrella Health and Welfare Agency (HWA), a "superagency" which includes the departments of Aging, Alcohol and Drug Abuse, Developmental Services, Employment Development, Health Services, Mental Health, Rehabilitation, and Social Services. The Office of Migration and Refugee Affairs (OMRA) coordinates all nonfederally reimbursed refugee program components. It provides staff support for the Governor's Refugee Task Force and Citizens Advisory Committee. OMRA also is responsible for developing the State Master Plan for Refugee Resettlement, which is separate from the Department of Social Services (DSS) State Plan for Refugee/Entrant Assistance and Services.

The DSS supervises the AFDC and food stamp programs, and monitors the federally administered Supplemental Security Income/State Supplementary Program (SSI/SSP). It is also responsible for supervising Title XX social services and the economic assistance and support services programs provided for refugees through county welfare departments and public and private service providers. The director of DSS is designated as the Refugee Services Coordinator.

Responsibility for managing and coordinating the state's refugee program rests in the Office of Refugee Services (ORS) within DSS. The ORS consists of three bureaus: County Welfare Operations, Contract Management, and Management Information and Planning.

The state's fifty-eight county welfare departments are responsible for processing refugee applications for assistance, for determining eligibility, for delivering benefits and services, and for making referrals to other agencies and service providers. County welfare departments also provide cash and medical assistance, and Title XX mandated services. County welfare departments may also contract with DSS for other services through a competitive process. The process is used by numerous private and public service providers to obtain funding for the provision of refugee support services.

California refugees are eligible for AFDC, state AFDC-U, and Refugee Cash Assistance (RCA). Food stamps, which are not reimbursed by ORR, are available to refugees on the same basis as nonrefugee residents. AFDC-U provides cash assistance to eligible families in which one parent is unemployed but does not meet the federal requirements for AFDC. A 1982 state law limits eligibility for benefits to no more than three months in any twelve-month period. Time-eligible refugees are provided assistance through RCA rather than AFDC-U. Only refugees who are time-expired for RCA and are not eligible for AFCD because they do not meet the federal requirements for contact with the labor force can receive assistance through AFDC-U.

Another state program that is available to California refugees who are ineligible for AFDC is the Emergency Assistance Program (EAP). This program provides cash assistance to intact families where both parents are unemployed and neither parent has a connection with the labor force. Eligibility for benefits is limited to no more than thirty days in any twelve-month period. Federal reimbursement is provided to the state for this program.

Refugees who are time-expired and are not eligible for AFDC may qualify for county General Assistance programs if they meet the same eligibility requirements as other citizens. These programs are funded entirely at the local level. They are administered by local governments, are not under the authority of DSS, and vary significantly from county to county.

The structural positioning of the Refugee Coordinator, as head of the DSS, and the large refugee population with its attendant problems, has made the refugee program an important political issue in California. The state legislature has taken an active interest in the program, setting limits on how funds should be allocated and establishing categories of client priority. The philosophy behind the program is one of active state involvement in a wide range of services. Until FY81, refugees enjoyed a "blanket eligibility" status for any and all public services under the assumption that providing such a wide range of support services would lead to self-sufficiency for the refugees in the shortest possible time.

Unfortunately, federal budget cuts in the Title XX Social Services Block Grant Program reduced the amount of federal funds that were available for the provision of support services, and county welfare departments were unable to cover the reductions.

The state legislature responded by limiting the refugee support service allocation of Title XX funds to a maximum of 35 percent of available federal funds. The remaining 65 percent was to be used for purchase-of-service agreements with private and public service contractors. The top priority for the allocation of these funds was given to ESL, particularly short-term, intensive, survival, and employment-oriented ESL. Second priority was given to employment services, and third priority to health services. Other services may be provided if funding is available.

The priority group of refugees is employable adults who are receiving or are likely to receive cash assistance. Within this group, first priority is given to those refugees who have the highest potential for becoming self-supporting and those with the greatest need. Top consideration is given to refugees who have been in the United States for thirty-six months or less but are ineligible for RCA as a result of the eighteen-month change. Second consideration is given to time-expired refugees. Third consideration is given to refugees who are closest to becoming time-expired.

Cuts in funding for Title XX services have also forced the state to restrict the types of support service programs that county welfare departments are mandated to administer. Beginning in FY82–83, each county is required to submit a county plan detailing the types and levels of services to be provided. Seven types of services are allowed. These include ESL, employment services, health accessing, social adjustment, mental health–related services, vocational ESL (VESL), and vocational training. County plans are then combined into fifteen regional plans. DSS uses these plans to develop a Services Delivery System, contracting with a mix of public and private service providers through competitive bidding.

Under the system, central intake units conduct initial refugee processing. Agencies acting as central intake units determine eligibility for ESL, vocational training, VESL, and employment services. To be eligible for vocational training and VESL, refugees must also meet federal program requirements regarding income and resource limitations.

Central intake units then determine client priority status and level of employability. There are three such levels. Level 1 includes refugees who are unemployed, have English-speaking skills, and need only employment-related services. Level 2 includes refugees who need some but not all of the four services. Level 3 includes refugees who are classified as employable, but in need of all four services.

Finally, central intake units develop job plans for refugees, and refer them to appropriate service providers. The providers are contracted for a maximum of twelve months and are subjected to numerous restrictions. For example, ESL instruction is limited to preliterate and survival ESL. Class time must exceed twenty hours a week. VESL must be concurrent with vocational training, unless good cause can be shown for exception. Vocational training must reflect local job market needs, and should be consistent with the refugee's abilities. Employment services are limited to those refugees who meet the definition for employables, and providers must observe the priority levels. Employment services must include assessment, information and referral, job counseling, the development of an individual employability plan, employment orientation, job development and placement, and thirty-, sixty-, and ninety-day follow-ups.

FY84 marks the implementation of the new, federally funded Targeted Assistance Program that gives California counties more control over their resettlement efforts. The counties will receive the largest proportion of these funds, with thirteen receiving over half of the total.[5] Los Angeles County alone will receive $6,995,319.

The move to local control of targeted assistance funds has prompted some criticisms.[6] Santa Clara County, which received $2.4 million in FY84, has been criticized by a twenty-two-member advisory committee that was established to make recommendations on the allocation of these funds. It criticized the on-the-job training emphasis as insensitive to social adjustment problems and cited a need for job skills training prior to employment. The Santa Clara plan has been criticized for duplicating already available services. Los Angeles County has been criticized by an advisor to the county for bypassing Indochinese mutual assistance associations and voluntary agencies in their distribution of funds. Finally, DSS has complained that this and other federal policy changes have placed it in a reactive position. It is not able to implement programs on its own initiative.

In sum, California's refugee program, with its mix of private and public service providers and emphasis on local initiative in developing service delivery plans, varies from county to county. The large size of the refugee population, their geographic dispersion, and variation in refugee needs and service providers have blocked the development of a unified state program. The use of a competitive bidding process has often resulted in county welfare departments and voluntary agencies competing for the same social service contracts and funding. The mixed system of private and public service provision has also resulted in duplication of services, competition for authority, and a lack of coordination and accountability. For the most part, however, it appears that the mix of private and public service providers works well, creating an interlocking network which attempts to utilize the particular skills and experiences of the agencies involved.

Texas

Texas has the second largest Indochinese refugee population in the United States. Official federal estimates were 57,700 as of September 1984. However, the Texas state government has claimed that this seriously underestimates the number of secondary migrants and that the refugee population is actually in the neighborhood of 85,000.[7] About 86 percent of these are Vietnamese, many of whom arrived as part of the first wave of 1975–76. Texas has, until recently, enjoyed strong economic growth and has a temperate climate, both significant factors in secondary migration. The influx of refugees has led to some community tensions over competition for jobs, housing, and resources, as well as cultural misunderstandings.

Federal budget cuts, mandated under the Omnibus Budget Reconciliation Act of 1981, affected Texas's social services programs by reducing Title XX funding by $23 million for FY82. Staffing in the Department of Human Resources was reduced by 849 positions, including the elimination of all bilingual staff in the state's resettlement program. As with most of the other states, these budget cuts led to an emphasis on refugee self-sufficiency in the shortest possible time, through the linkage of ESL and employment services. Approximately one-third of the total allocation of funding for refugee programs was set aside for ESL and employment services. Specific guidelines were set for all ESL classes across the state in an effort to standardize instruction. In most cases the same service providers also were responsible for vocational training, although under separate contracts. Employment services were provided primarily by local service providers, both public and private, with an emphasis on job placement. Texas sets targeted levels for projected job placements for each year. Social services were directed mainly to support those refugees in ESL and job placement programs.

The Department of Human Resources (DHR) is the designated state agency for the administration of the refugee program. The Board of Human Resources oversees the direction, policy, and performance of DHR. The board's three members are appointed by the governor and confirmed by the state senate. The board selects the DHR Commissioner, who is responsible for the administration of DHR programs. There are five deputy commissioners and a number of associate commissioners. The associate commissioner for the Administration for Services to Families and Children is the designated coordinator for refugee programs. The state coordinator spends about 25 percent of his time on the refugee program.[8]

The state is divided into twelve regions that correspond to the state's twelve health service areas. The regional contract managers have considerable responsibility for refugee program design decisions. Within each region, DHR contracts with a variety of private and public service providers for refugee services.

The governor, through the governor's liaison office, maintains an active interest in the refugee program. There is a 167-member Governor's Task Force which meets infrequently, although individual members are frequently consulted. Refugee issues are specifically addressed by the twenty-four member Refugee Resettlement Advisory Council, whose members are appointed by the governor. Its membership consists of refugees, representatives of local government, voluntary agencies, and service providers. There is also a Governor's Liaison for Voluntary Assistance which has been actively involved in the formation of local task forces in Dallas and Houston, two of the largest resettlement areas. Personal contacts and informal interagency agreements appear to be the major mechanisms for coordinating the activities of the resettlement program.[9]

Since the Texas legislature meets biennially, DHR budget requests are for two-year periods. DHR submits an official request for funds in July of each even-numbered year. In the spring of odd-numbered years the legislature develops two-year appropriations for the agency. These funds are then allocated to each region along historical lines. Each region develops a service delivery plan which is then submitted and negotiated with state program office staff. Responsibility for financial management of the refugee program is shared between the refugee program offices and the Budget Planning and Management Support Unit of DHR.

The refugee office is responsible for development of income maintenance policy and oversees the delivery of cash and medical assistance. There are no formal mechanisms for service referrals for refugees, and there is no designated agency that has responsibility for providing cash management functions. The decentralized nature of the regional planning system has contributed to a program which is similar in nature to California's, with contracts awarded to a mix of public and private service providers. The program is not unified.

Refugees are entitled to AFDC, SSI, Title XX programs, and Refugee Cash Assistance and Medical Assistance. Texas does not have an AFDC-U program, nor does it have statewide General Assistance programs. In those counties with some type of General Assistance, refugees who are considered employable are not eligible for benefits. AFDC payments in FY82 averaged $34.52 a month per person, the second lowest in the country. Per capita social service expenditures for refugees is about $116, compared to about $500 for California. These comparatively low rates of expenditure and benefits have evidently been balanced out by high rates of employment and an expanding Texas economy. The dependency rate for refugees in Texas is one of the lowest among the states. In contrast, California has consistently had one of the highest dependency rates, averaging about 60 percent.

Assistance programs in Texas combine a number of federal funding sources to meet broadly defined goals. Refugee Resettlement Program services fall under the Family Self-Support Program. The Family Self-Support Program "provides services to help families become self-supporting and self-sufficient by assisting clients to meet their income and health needs."[10] Priority services provided to refugees are ESL with an emphasis on survival English related to employment, employment services including career counseling, job plan development, job orientation and placement, and vocational training. ESL and employment services are provided to refugees without regard to income.

Priority in service provision is given to those refugees receiving cash assistance. These services include information and referral, outreach, assessment and service planning, translation and interpreter services, home management services, skills recertification, and transportation, when necessary for employment-related activities. The state also contracts with agencies to provide for unaccompanied refugee minors. Health services include referral, counseling, and assistance in making appointments and obtaining services. In addition, the Texas Department of Health monitors those refugees identified by the federal government as having a history of problems or conditions requiring treatment or observation. The low rates of dependency and utilization of these services are indicated by a total social services caseload of about 6,000 refugees, or 10 percent of the official refugee population.

All refugees who are AFDC recipients are required to register for a work incentive program if they live within a program area. The requirement does not apply statewide. Work incentive services focus on employment and include social support services to assist refugees in obtaining and retaining employment. Employment services are provided by the Texas Employment Commission, while support services are provided by DHR. These support services are provided for thirty days following the acceptance of unsubsidized employment and may be continued for up to ninety days. Support services may be continued even if the individual is denied AFDC because of employment.

Refugees are also eligible for most other Title XX services if they are AFDC, SSI, or RCA recipients, or if they meet Title XX income eligibility requirements. These requirements are based on the state median income for a family of four, which is $23,416. The income eligibility criteria is set at 47 percent of the median income as adjusted for family size. DHR also participates in community-based pilot projects, on a special project basis, to encourage self-support. These services are also contracted to a mix of public and private agencies.

Washington

The refugee population of Washington was estimated at 32,700 as of September 1984. As with most of the other states with large refugee populations, Washington has been involved in refugee resettlement since 1975. A well established nonrefugee Asian community in Seattle has provided a support network for refugee arrivals. King County, in which Seattle is located, has the state's highest concentration of refugees, with a population of 19,000. Washington has a high unemployment rate, with Seattle being particularly hard hit by recent economic conditions. The limited job market, combined with the fact that the state's General Assistance programs are not available to employees, has resulted in a fairly high rate of out-migration. A large percentage of its Hmong population has moved to California's central valley or to Texas in search of employment opportunities. High rates of unemployment and public assistance dependency, along with an anticipated continued decline in federal funding, have led Washington to revise and restructure much of its refugee program for 1984.

The Bureau of Refugee Assistance (BORA) is a separate bureau within the Department of Social and Health Services. It was formerly a unit of the Children's Services Bureau. The move has increased the political visibility of the bureau and allowed it to operate more effectively.[11] The state office is one of the few that have made an effort to utilize bilingual refugees as program staff. The state office also has a full-time Refugee Coordinator.

Beginning in 1984, BORA will be using a block grant funding procedure for contracting for service provision. Under this procedure, BORA will contract with one organizational entity in each area having a high concentration of refugees, and that entity will be responsible for allocating the block grant money to local service providers. If no such entity exists, BORA will contract directly with the local service providers. Competitive bids are not mandatory in awarding these contracts. This represents a departure from BORA's previous practice of contracting directly with local providers. The block grant program is intended as a more flexible approach that will be more responsive to local needs.

The allocation formula for social service funds has also been changed for 1984. Previously Washington state allocated funds to localities based upon the distribution of refugees. The 1984 plan cites four major problems with that approach: (1) the number of refugees in a locality and the number of refugees in need may not be the same; (2) there are no accurate means of determining the total number of refugees in a locality; (3) the formulas do not reflect the need for funding or allow for the availability of special funding such as targeted assistance; and (4) the formulas do not take into account the performance, initiative, or special needs of localities. The new formula is based on population in need, defined as the number of refugees who have been in the United States for less than eighteen months and the number of recipients of Refugee Cash Assistance and AFDC. Those counties that are recipients of special funding will have their allocation level reduced. The amount of the reduction will be held in a "reserve fund" that will be either reallocated if it is necessary to continue service provision, or awarded to counties based upon demonstrated performance, local initiative, or special need. Future allocations will be increasingly based on performance in fostering employment.

The organizational criteria for funding are fairly open, as long as the contracted agency meets certain minimum criteria. Two services must be provided: employment services and ESL classes. Other services are optional, but are expected to be employment-related. Initial reception, placement, and orientation will continue to be provided by voluntary agencies, and such services will not be considered reimbursable by BORA. A minimum of 40 percent of allocated social service funds must be spent on the two required services. BORA estimates that the actual figure should be about 85 percent. A needs assessment must be included as part of the local service plan. This must include information regarding refugee needs in the area and how provided services will respond to these needs. Coordination and sharing of information among service providers is necessary to ensure consistency in the overall refugee program and to avoid duplication of services and information.

BORA has established a client priority classification similar to those of Texas and California. However, the criteria for client eligibility are more flexible than those of the other two states and leave the specification of additional eligibility or priority factors up to the local agency. Special emphasis is given to the "hard to place." These are refugees considered employable but who require special efforts for placement. The definition of the "hard to place" is vague and is left up to the local planning agency. Each county plan is expected to address this issue and to specify actions for meeting the needs of this group.

The employment services that are provided are also similar to those provided by California and Texas. BORA will determine a specific number of placements that each county must achieve. Job placement is defined as a job held by the individual for at least thirty days which pays the equivalent of a forty-hour week at minimum wage. Providers will be required to do a ninety-day follow-up on employed clients.

BORA has an interagency agreement with the Superintendent of Public Instruction for language services. This has resulted in a comprehensive ESL program and a state ESL master plan. All eligible refugees in need of ESL services are to have access to ESL instruction within funding limitations. ESL instruction is standardized and competency-based, with student progress monitored at quarterly intervals and evaluated through various procedures. Instruction is limited to 540 hours unless special need can be shown. Average class size has been reduced from twenty students to fifteen. Wherever possible, volunteers are to be utilized as teaching staff.

BORA has made a special effort to involve Indochinese Mutual Assistance Associations (IMAAS) as service providers. Recognizing the difficulty that IMAAS have in competing against more established service providers, BORA has awarded separate contracts to IMAAS and required them to build coalitions to increase the cost effectiveness, competitiveness, and availability of services to all refugees. A minimum of 7 percent of allocated funds are to be set aside for IMAAS. BORA will provide staff from the Office of Refugee Community Development to act as technical advisors to IMAAS. Activities considered eligible for reimbursement are restricted to services related to resettlement and the achievement of refugee self-sufficiency. Traditional activities of IMAAS that are cultural, religious, and social are not eligible for reimbursement.

As a result of the reduction in the eligibility period for refugees from thirty-six to eighteen months, nearly 10,000 refugees were dropped from Washington's resettlement programs in June 1982. BORA conducted a study to determine the effects of these terminations.[12] The study found that three months after the terminations, about 47 percent of the households had earned income from the employment of the head and/or spouse. Sixteen percent had not earned any income but were receiving some form of cash assistance. Twenty-six percent were receiving food stamps, but had no earned income or cash assistance. Eleven percent had no earned income, were receiving no cash assistance, and were not receiving food stamps. Of those in the labor force, 29 percent were employed full-time, 21 percent were employed part-time, and 50 percent were unemployed.

Ten months after termination, 55 percent of the refugee households were self-supporting. Of those in the labor force, 60 percent were employed full- or part-time, an increase of 10 percent. The Hmong had the hardest time following termination, and the highest rate of out-migration. Between February 1982 and April 1983, over 18 percent of the refugees in the sample moved out of state. Over 50 percent of these were Hmong. The Hmong also had the lowest level of English language skills, despite having the highest level of ESL exposure of any refugee ethnic group.

Pennsylvania

Pennsylvania was one of the states that acted as an initial receiving center for refugees. Fort Indiantown Gap, near Harrisburg, opened 28 May 1975. Sixteen thousand first-wave refugees were processed here. As a result, Pennsylvania has the third largest Vietnamese population, after California and Texas. The state is unusual in that its refugee population is fairly evenly distributed across the state rather than concentrated in a few areas. The refugee population, officially estimated at 23,888, constitutes only about 0.2 percent of the state's total population.

The Pennsylvania refugee program was originally located within the Office of Income Maintenance, then moved to the Office of Social Programs. When this office was disbanded, the program moved to its present location within the Office of Children, Youth and Families. These moves all took place within the Department of Public Welfare and were apparently accomplished with little disruption to the program. The Department of Public Welfare is the designated resettlement agency, and the Secretary of Public Welfare is the State Coordinator for refugee resettlement. Eligiblity of refugees for services and program accountability are handled by the same state units that handle mainstream public welfare programs.

Refugee social service contracts are awarded to service providers within Pennsylvania's four regions through a competitive bidding process. There is one full-time refugee program manager for southeast Pennsylvania. The remaining three regions contract for refugee social services by including the appropriate provisions in their mainstream social service contracts. These four regional Refugee Program Managers have a major input into the design and implementation of refugee services. There is also a Refugee Advisory Council, which meets infrequently.

Prior to 1982, Pennsylvania provided one of the widest ranges of social service that states offered to refugees. 1982 funding cuts of 60 percent forced a reduction in available services from twenty-four to five. The services that remain include case management/service planning, employment services, ESL classes, translation/interpretation, and vocational training. Eliminated services include day care, family planning, outreach, and information and referral. Services are generally oriented towards new arrivals and public assistance recipients. Income eligibility requirements have been tightened from 90 percent to 50 percent of the state's median income.

Employment services are provided by a variety of public and private service providers, with contracts awarded through a competitive bidding process. Vocational training must be offered for a minimum of six hours a day, five days a week, and is limited to six months per individual. Agencies providing vocational training must also provide job placement and follow-up. ESL is limited to 1000 hours for each individual, but cannot exceed eighteen consecutive months. ESL is provided by both private and mainstream public service providers.

Illinois

Illinois has the fifth largest Indochinese refugee population. Most of the state's 22,000 refugees are concentrated in the Cook County area, which includes Chicago. Refugee and immigrant resettlement is not new to Chicago. It also has large concentrations of Polish, Russian, Greek, and Latin immigrants and refugees.

The Illinois Department of Public Aid (IDPA) is the designated state agency for developing and administering the refugee program.[13] The program is located within the Bureau of Social Services, and the Chief of the Bureau is designated as the refugee resettlement coordinator. The Refugee Resettlement Program (RRP) office is responsible for planning, administration, coordination, and technical assistance.

Three of its Social Service Planner positions are bilingual. One combines Lao and Hmong, and the others are Cambodian and Vietnamese.

There are two prime contractors for social service provision. The Jewish Federation/Chicago Refugee Social Services Consortium (CRSSC) includes fourteen service provider offices that provide employment and adjustment services. The Northwestern Educational Cooperative/Adult Indochinese Refugee Consortium (AIRC) includes fifteen service provider offices, is statewide, and excludes Chicago. AIRC's emphasis is on ESL and includes employment and adjustment services.

Case management is provided by the agency that provides employment services. In Chicago, the voluntary agencies may operate as job placement agencies or refer the refugee to another agency that has been contracted to provide employment services. When the voluntary agency refers the refugee to another agency, the voluntary agency maintains responsibility for follow-up and case resolution. Secondary migrants are assigned to a voluntary agency by the Department of Public Aid. Refugees who live outside of the Chicago area register with an AIRC provider in their area or, if none exists, with Illinois Job Services. The Department of Public Aid estimates that 90 percent of Illinois's refugees have access to programs that are refugee-specific. Refugees are informed of such programs through various channels such as voluntary agencies, ethnic language newspapers, and Indochinese mutual assistance agencies.

Voluntary agencies and other refugee service providers were recognized as authorized case management agencies in July 1981 in a move to increase the cooperation and communication between service providers and the Department of Public Aid. The move gave service providers more input into program design and increased authority to levy sanctions against refugees who refuse appropriate offers of employment. First priority in service delivery is ESL and employment services, with refugees on cash assistance given priority for receipt of services. New arrivals, principally those who have lived in the United States for less than one year, are given second priority.

Because of the decentralized nature of the state's service delivery system, Illinois conducts an extensive needs assessment for each individual refugee. These assessments are generally conducted by bilingual staff who attempt to assess native language ability, English language ability, employability, vocational experience, and aptitude. Jewish Vocational Service and Truman College are responsible for the vocational assessment of most refugees in the Chicago area. Outside of Chicago, needs assessments are conducted by contracted educational service providers.

Medical and health services are provided through the Illinois Department of Public Health (IDPH). IDPH has established an Indochinese Health Assessment Program which identifies new arrivals whose medical condition or history indicates the need for continued observation or treatment. In FY82, 7.5 percent of the state's social service funding was allocated for bilingual staffing for health services. The remainder of the social service funding is divided between the two service provider consortia in accordance with the state's distribution of refugees. Currently half goes to the RSSC in Chicago and half goes to the AIRC. Both groups distribute funds to service providers through a competitive bidding process.

Unaccompanied minors are handled by the Illinois Department of Children and Family Services (DCFS). DCFS has designated a Refugee Program Coordinator within the Programs Operations division of the Central Office. Peoria Catholic Social Services has been contracted by DCFS to establish a reception center where unaccompanied refugee minors receive needs assessments and orientation. Unaccompanied minors are placed with foster parents on a case by case basis. A number of unaccompanied refugee minors have entered communities on their own, without legal guardians or sponsors. DCFS is attempting to identify these children and provide services for them either through purchase of service agreements with private agencies or through direct placement in foster homes.

Minnesota

Minnesota has over 22,000 Indochinese refugees. These refugees are highly visible, as they constitute a significant proportion of the state's small Asian population. The state has been involved in resettlement since 1975, with the major portion of refugees arriving in 1979 and 1980. The Minnesota refugee population is unique in that it includes about 40 percent of the total Hmong population. The large number of Hmong, who are from rural backgrounds, often illiterate in their own language, have very little formal education, and possess few skills that are transferable to a technological society, pose significant and unique problems for Minnesota. Ramsey County, which includes part of the Twin Cities area, has the largest concentration of refugees, about 80 percent of whom are Hmong. Half of these are secondary migrants.

The designated state resettlement agency is the Minnesota Department of Public Welfare. The Refugee Program Office is located within the Bureau of Income Maintenance. The staff of the Refugee Program Office consists of the State Coordinator and refugee program specialists in the areas of employment, housing, legal and community relations, administration and finance, health, education and training, and contract management. This office establishes purchase of service agreements for the provision of refugee services. It currently contracts with over fifty public and private agencies. Other services are provided by county welfare departments and the state Departments of Education and Health.

Additional groups involved in resettlement include the State Refugee Advisory Council, the Mutual Assistance Association Advisory Council, and the Minnesota Consortium for Refugee Resettlement. Local neighborhood organizations have also been organized to deal with community issues in areas of high impact. The Ramsey County Planning Team and the Minneapolis Mayor's Forum have been particularly effective. Specific program areas are dealt with by special committees. These are the State Health Advisory Committee on Refugees, the Refugee Education Task Force, and the Employment Vendor Council. Ad hoc committees may be formed to deal with issues as they arise.

Area Coordinating Centers were established in areas outside of the Twin Cities in 1979, in response to the high concentration of refugees in the Twin Cities. These centers have implemented programs to stimulate the movement of refugees out of the Twin Cities area.

Minnesota's Refugee Program Office has taken an active role in encouraging and soliciting support from the private sector for resettlement program needs. In 1982 a limited health interpreter program was funded by private foundations. Under the program, an interpreter accompanies the refugee to a health assessment and explains the results of the assessment. The interpreters are needed because most health care facilities do not have their own bilingual staff. Indeed, one of the objectives of the State Health Department is the incorporation of trained health interpreters into the permanent personnel programs of health care institutions. These institutions have already made a significant effort to provide interpretation, absorbing costs of over $349,000 previously funded through federal refugee social service money.

Assessment of the medical condition and needs of incoming refugees is conducted at selected public facilities in the metropolitan area and through the offices of private physicians participating in the program in rural areas. The eighteen-month limitation has reduced the number of refugees using available health services.

There has been recent concern in Minnesota over the increasing incidence of spouse and child abuse, and attempted suicide. In an effort to deal with these problems, Minnesota is utilizing direct educational and counseling services provided by Asian personnel to provide culturally appropriate and acceptable services.

Ninety percent of the total social service budget is allocated to employment services and ESL. Approximately 75 percent of this funding is allocated for employment-related ESL and basic skills. Educational objectives have been developed for the four levels of ESL instruction with the goal of preparing refugees for employment in the shortest possible time. Time limits have been established for each of the four levels of instruction, for a total of 1500 hours. Services are contracted through a competitive bid process to a mix of public and private service providers.

Priority target populations for ESL training services and employment services are similar to those of other states. Minnesota's inclusion of the needs of refugee women is a unique recognition of the problems of this group, and of their potential to become economic contributors to the household. ESL guidelines are standardized, with services provided at each of the four levels of instruction and delivered in a variety of formats geared to the different needs of the target populations. In 1983 Minnesota expanded its language efforts to provide ESL instruction to those refugees already employed or engaged in full-time job search. This includes the provision of part-time and evening instruction, and, through cooperative agreements with employers, job site instruction.

Employment programs, in order of priority, are employability assessment and plan development, job development, placement and follow-up, short-term "world of work" orientation, employment progress monitoring, employment counseling, job upgrading services, and innovative programs that would lead directly to refugee employment within three months. Flexibility in funding is achieved by considering the employment needs, population concentrations, and location of adult refugees rather than maintaining existing programs. Innovative, replicable, and low-cost programs are encouraged, as is the use of other public and private funding sources. The State Refugee Program Office exerts a strong influence on the design of programs and has established mechanisms that assure accountability and adherence to Program Office guidelines.

Minnesota also participates in the unaccompanied minors program. Two voluntary agencies, Catholic Charities and Lutheran Social Services, negotiate with each county regarding the placement and care of unaccompanied refugee minors. Legal custody is established through the court of the county in which the minor resides. This does not terminate parental rights, thereby ensuring that the minor will not be eligible for adoption. Placement is directly into foster care homes. To the extent possible, the agencies attempt to place the child in a home with a similar cultural, religious, and ethnic background.

Conclusions

Federal funding changes and continued uncertainty over funding levels have forced states to reconsider their refugee resettlement program designs and to increase the emphasis on employment, program coordination, and accountability. Voluntary agencies have expanded their role to include case management, referral, and employment services as well as their traditional role in initial resettlement. Social services have been greatly reduced. The decision to limit eligibility for ORR reimbursement to eighteen months has created financial hardships for county General Assistance programs. This has been a major factor in the state decisions to limit refugee programs to those that provide ESL and employment-related services. The linking of ESL and employment services reflects the widely held perception that English language ability is directly related to employment success.

5
Living
Conditions
and
Adjustment

Despite the emphasis of government programs and policies, little is known about the general characteristics of the Indochinese refugee population. Basic questions have not been answered by the scant studies that have been conducted. How are they living? How are they adapting? What are their basic living arrangements? Most studies have been limited to the presentation of demographic profiles or to one ethnic group, most often the Vietnamese. The study on which this book is based remedies some of the deficiencies of previous studies by offering a detailed analysis of all the ethnic groups involved in the Indochinese resettlement effort.

In this chapter we discuss the major characteristics of the Indochinese refugees living in one resettlement site. The site is San Diego, California. San Diego is an excellent site for studying the resettlement experiences of Indochinese refugees because most refugees have resettled in a relatively small number of urban areas, several of which are in California. Of the over 700,000 refugees who have resettled in the United States since April 1975, approximately 260,000 live in California, and an estimated 42,000 live in San Diego.

Before exploring the living conditions of this group, we will delineate the research design and sampling procedures used in the survey of 800 San Diego area Indochinese refugees. There are many survey and sampling obstacles involved in the study. Caution in the interpretation of results can be exercised only with an understanding of how the study surmounts these obstacles.

Questionnaire and Study Design

A number of atypical interviewing problems were anticipated in the
study and were addressed in the development of the questionnaire.
First, it was assumed that respondents would be reluctant to answer
some of the more important questions, given their uncertain residency status and lack of exposure to U.S. political and judicial customs. Second, it was assumed that the cultural backgrounds of refugee families would interfere with the identification of respondents
who would be most capable of providing useful information on the
economic self-support aspect of the resettlement experience. Third,
because respondents could not be assumed to be proficient in
English, the questionnaire had to be translated into Vietnamese, Lao,
and Cambodian.

In order to minimize the risk of including items that would be
offensive to respondents or excluding items relevant to assessing
refugee needs, an advisory committee was established to review
early drafts of the questionnaire. This committee was composed of
representatives from the San Diego Community College District's ESL
program, local Indochinese Mutual Assistance Associations, voluntary agencies, the County Welfare Department's Indochinese Orientation and Employment Program, the state's Employment Development Department, and local private refugee service providers.
Community leaders from each of the four major ethnic groups were
included on the committee in one or another of these capacities.
The committee held five monthly meetings to review the drafts of
the questionnaire and recommended five major revisions. Their recommendations are reflected in the final draft of the questionnaire,
included as appendix B at the end of this book.

The final draft of the English language version of the questionnaire was translated into Lao, Cambodian, and Vietnamese by experienced translators. These translations were then reviewed by a
second team of translators. When a disagreement in translation
occurred, a third translator was consulted and the item was discussed until a consensus was reached on item syntax and seman-
tics. Finally, the interpreters were asked to review both the English
and the primary language versions of the questionnaire to determine whether or not the versions conveyed the same information. If disagreement appeared at this stage, a discussion of the

item was reopened until a consensus once again was established.

The questionnaire was designed to be administered to one member of each household. Given the policy emphasis on economic self-support, it was decided that the most appropriate person to interview would be the person who is primarily responsible for the self-support of the household. However, this person may not always be considered by members of the household to be the head of household, particularly in cases where the oldest male in the household is handicapped or unemployed. In order to avoid offending the head of household in a situation where cultural norms require deferment to head of household, the interviewers were instructed to make initial contact with the culturally designated head of household and to determine, through open-ended conversation, the household member most responsible for the self-support of the household. If the head of household was not the member most responsible for self-support, the interviewer identified another household member to be interviewed.

In addition to providing extensive information on the household member designated to be responsible for the household's economic self-support, the questionnaire provided information on all other household members. This information was not extensive, but included employment status, demographics, and awareness and utilization of resettlement services. It was assumed that this information would provide a valuable insight into employment barriers related to sex, age, and family structure.

Sampling Strategy

The primary obstacle in identifying the San Diego Indochinese refugee population was the absence of a complete, reliable, current, and accessible population list. Recognizing this constraint, three criteria were used to evaluate alternative population lists. First, the list had to be current in order to include current addresses for early arrivals, recent arrivals, and secondary migrants. Second, the list could not systematically exclude certain groups of refugees such as secondary migrants, those who are employed, or those who arrived recently. Third, the list had to be accessible. Some lists are protected by the Privacy Act and could not be released.

A variety of sampling strategies were considered in light of these criteria. Among them were Immigration and Naturalization Service (INS) alien registration files, ESL class rosters, Indochinese Mutual Assistance Association membership rosters, private service provider participant lists, Indochinese Orientation and Employment Program participant lists, agency user lists, and the local telephone directory.

The Indochinese Orientation and Employment Program (IOEP) is operated by the San Diego County Welfare Department. It consists primarily of job counseling and job placement services. Refugees who apply for public assistance are required to enroll in IOEP as a condition of receiving the assistance. Although participation in IOEP (current and past) is believed to be quite high, the use of these files as a population list would systematically undersample refugees who are self-sufficient. Self-sufficient refugees would not be included in current IOEP files. And, though they may be included in closed IOEP files, these files would not likely include current addresses or telephone numbers. Furthermore, closed files would likely include refugees who are no longer living in the San Diego area.

As refugees are eligible to receive a number of services from private service providers, private service provider client lists were also considered as a possible population list from which to draw a sample. However, these lists were rejected because they would undersample refugees who are not currently receiving services. In addition, private service provider lists are subject to duplication as refugees can receive services simultaneously from a number of different providers.

Indochinese Mutual Assistance Associations (IMAA) are organizations that are composed of and managed by refugees. Many refugees are believed to join these organizations in order to exchange information on resettlement experiences and obtain resettlement information from members of their own ethnic community. Each major ethnic group has at least one IMAA organization. The Vietnamese community includes a number of them. However, the extent to which IMAA membership lists were complete was assumed to vary considerably from one ethnic group to another. The Vietnamese lists were assumed to be the least complete. Because the Vietnamese represent a larger proportion of San Diego's Indochinese refugee community, and because it was impossible to determine the difference between IMAA members and nonmembers, a decision was made not to use the IMAA lists.

User lists from the voluntary agencies were considered but were found to be dated and exclusive of secondary migrants. These agencies are responsible for the initial resettlement of refugees. After initial resettlement, refugees are directed to other agencies to obtain further assistance and services. Since early arrivals may have relocated after their last voluntary agency contact and since secondary migrants will not always have contacted a local voluntary agency, the use of agency lists would result in an undersampling of early arrivals and secondary migrants. This is the primary reason for rejecting voluntary agency files as a primary population list.

Current and past ESL class rosters were considered as a potential population list because the classes are widely attended by Indochinese refugees. In addition, ESL class rosters were assumed to include representative samples of secondary migrants and recent arrivals. Although the addresses of early arrivals on past ESL rosters were not expected to be current, this was not the primary reason for rejecting the rosters as a population list. An extensive review of ESL class rosters indicated that the procedure for storing participant information had changed in 1978. Prior to 1978, re-enrollment would appear as a multiple entry in the list. This practice would make it very difficult to ensure that each refugee had an equal probability of being included in a sample. Furthermore, the rosters often included persons who were not refugees.

The telephone directory was considered and ultimately selected as a population list. The major problem posed by the use of the directory was completeness. If refugees did not generally have access to a telephone, a population list generated from the telephone directory would not be representative of the entire population. If they did have access, the telephone directory could be assumed to be current, as it is revised every year. It could also be assumed to be nonexclusive of secondary migrants or early arrivals because migration or arrival status are not criteria for obtaining a telephone.

The issue of access was investigated by reviewing service provider lists. These lists included data on telephone access. The review indicated that approximately 90 percent of the refugees on these lists were able to give a current telephone number. Recent arrivals were given special attention in this regard because they were assumed to be the least likely to have access to a telephone. In this case, representatives from local voluntary agency offices indicated that most recent arrivals had telephones because telephones were considered necessary for communication. Indeed, installation deposits for telephones were often subsidized by voluntary agencies.

The only remaining problem with the use of the telephone directory was the inclusion of the most recent arrivals. The most recent telephone directory available at the time of the study (June 1981) was published in January 1981 and included new listings through October 1980. Arrivals between November 1980 and June 1981 could not possibly be included in the telephone directory. This problem was resolved by obtaining, from each area voluntary agency, the number of refugees that had resettled between December 1980 and June 1981. This number was then figured as a proportion of the estimated number of refugees living in San Diego at the time. By these calculations, approximately 10 percent of the San Diego refugee population had arrived between November 1980 and June 1981. The same proportion was included in the final sample of 800 by randomly selecting 80 respondents from voluntary agency lists of refugees who had been resettled between November 1980 and June 1981. Thus, the final sample included 720 respondents drawn from the telephone directory and 80 respondents drawn from voluntary agency lists of refugees who had been resettled since November 1980. The only refugees excluded by this technique were secondary migrants who arrived in San Diego after November 1980 without contacting a voluntary agency, and refugees who had no telephone or an unlisted telephone number. Given the alternatives, this approach was determined to be the least biased.

The process of extracting names, addresses, and telephone numbers of refugees from the telephone directory was simplified by the fact that their names are easily identifiable according to the ethnic group to which they belong. Accordingly, the translators of the survey instruments were also instructed to review every entry in the telephone direcrectory and record each entry from the ethnic group for which they were translating. The results of each review were verified on a random basis for completeness. The resulting lists were maintained as separate ethnic group files. It was assumed that each entry would represent one household and at least one family unit (more than one family unit would be represented in cases where different families share the same household and telephone). The results of the sampling procedure, the composition of the final sample, and response rates are given in table 5.1.

Table 5.1 Sampling procedure results

	Vietnamese	Lao	Hmong	Cambodian	Overall
Attempted	644	203	114	144	1105
Completed	430	160	100	110	800
Completed: telephone list	397	140	90	93	720
Completed: voluntary agency	33	20	10	17	80
Refusals	55	2	2	3	62
Disconnects	59	4	1	7	71
Moved	47	24	3	7	81
Unable to contact[a]	53	13	8	17	91
Completion rate: percentage attempted	65.7%	78.8%	87.7%	76.4%	72.3%
Completion rate: percentage completed	87.2%	98.7%	98.0%	97.3%	92.3%

a. After four attempts to make telephone contact.

The major considerations in maintaining quality interviewing for this survey were the selection and training of interviewers, the identification and establishment of trust among the proper respondents, and the validation of survey results. Interviewers were required to be proficient in English as well as the language of the households they were assigned to interview. They were also required to attend training sessions on survey research and interviewing techniques. The validation of survey results was done through telephone interviews conducted by independent bilingual interviewers. Interviewing and validating were totally independent processes.

Basic Demographic Profile

The basic demographic profile of the refugee sample is assumed to reflect the profile for the general population of refugees. However, since the interviews were with the head of household, the percentage of women who were interviewed is relatively low.

Age. The age distributions of the heads of households indicates a relatively young population. As table 5.2 indicates, the average age is thirty-seven years. Only 17 percent of the refugee heads are under twenty-seven years of age and 9 percent are fifty-five years of age or

Table 5.2   Age of head of household by ethnicity (in percent)

Age (in years)	Vietnamese	Lao	Hmong	Cambodian	Overall
0–27	18.1	14.4	23.0	11.8	17.1
28–35	30.2	34.4	38.0	37.3	33.0
36–44	24.4	31.9	18.0	24.5	25.1
45–54	16.3	16.3	12.0	14.5	15.5
55–86	10.7	3.1	9.0	11.8	9.1
Don't know/no answer	0.2	0.0	0.0	0.0	0.1
$N =$	430	160	100	110	800
Mean age	38.0	36.6	35.7	39.3	37.6

older. The Cambodians tend to be older than the other ethnic groups, and the Hmong tend to be younger. Clearly, a majority of these refugees are relatively young, creating communities without clear patterns of authority between the young and the old.[1]

Household number and size. In our sample, the Vietnamese were the dominant refugee household for each year of arrival. The Laotians, Cambodians, and Hmong begin to appear in larger numbers after the end of the first wave.

The cultural dissimilarity between these refugees and American society is manifest in the size and composition of each household. The patriarchal tradition of Indochina places great emphasis on large nuclear families.[2] Studies by the U.S. Immigration and Naturalization Service reveal that the number of family groups who were able to flee Indochina together was remarkably high.[3] In our sample, we found the mean size of the nuclear family to be 4.46 persons and the mean household size to be 6.02 persons. In comparison with the American population, these figures are quite high.

Table 5.3   Mean household size by type of household and ethnicity of head

	Vietnamese	Lao	Hmong	Cambodian	Overall
Nuclear family	4.10	4.83	5.32	4.51	4.46
Extended family	0.90	1.73	2.71	0.83	1.29
Nonfamily	0.27	0.24	0.03	0.48	0.26
Mean household	5.28	6.81	8.07	5.84	6.02
Total	2246	1053	810	649	4758

The composition of each household varies according to the ethnic makeup of the household. The large extended family of the Hmong and Laotians is a carryover from the tribal nature of their culture. In most refugee households there are some nonfamily members. This finding can be attributed in part to the exigencies of forced migration. Large households offer some advantages in terms of resources. The cost of housing and the relatively low pay received by refugees provide an inducement to cluster. In addition, an extended family offers family members psychological comfort and cultural reinforcement.

Marital and reunification status. A high proportion of our respondents are married, and the number who are single heads of household is relatively small. Cambodians and Laotians have a large percent of widowed heads of household, 10 percent and 9 percent respectively. This is likely attributable to the rapid escalation of violence in Laos and Cambodia. Also, the perilous nature of land and sea exit from Cambodia has been noted by reports from refugee camps.[4] Family members were often separated in the rapidity of the migration, and many lost their lives in flight.

Reunification of family members has been an important goal of many refugee families. Efforts to relocate family members have been concerted. The developing refugee associations have been effective agents in helping families reunite. Table 5.4 provides basic data on the arrival conditions of heads of household by ethnicity. A high proportion of respondents were among the first in their family to settle in the United States. However, a large proportion of the Hmong, Cambodians, and Laotians were secondary migrants for the purpose of reunification. The arrival of these refugees can best be seen as due to pull factors as well as the push factors of forced migration.

Table 5.4 Arrival conditions of head of household by ethnicity (in percent)

	Vietnamese	Lao	Hmong	Cambodian	Overall
Among the first	77.9	55.6	34.0	40.9	62.9
Reunited	21.9	44.4	66.0	59.1	37.0
Don't know/no answer	0.2	0.0	0.0	0.0	0.1
N =	430	160	100	110	800

In summary, the basic demographic profile of these refugees tends to be different from other immigrants. They are younger, married, and have extended families which are being reunited in the United States. There are differences among ethnic groups on most demographic variables, reflecting heterogeneity of the refugee population. However, differences in prearrival conditions are also important in explaining how refugees in similar resettlement conditions differ in terms of resettlement experience.

Prearrival Conditions

The diversity and problems of Indochinese resettlement originate in the diversity of their prearrival environments. Naturally, some refugees are better prepared for resettlement than others, given their backgrounds. Further, the timing and the trauma of the migration have some effect on the ability of the refugee to adjust to the host society. The following variables and discussion give a picture of the diversity in prearrival conditions.

Prearrival education. The prearrival level of education is one indicator of the level of social development of the refugee's home environment. According to the data presented in table 5.5, a third of these refugees have received at least some high school education and only 17 percent have received no formal education. Overall, the level of education of these refugees should not be a major barrier to their adaptation to American life.

Table 5.5 Home country education of head of household by ethnicity (in percent)

	Vietnamese	Lao	Hmong	Cambodian	Overall
No formal education	14.0	13.8	41.0	11.8	17.0
Elementary or less	12.3	38.8	40.0	31.8	23.8
Some high school	33.5	31.3	18.0	52.7	33.8
High school graduate	12.1	11.9	1.0	2.7	9.4
Beyond high school	27.7	4.4	0.0	0.9	15.9
Don't know/no answer	0.5	0.0	0.0	0.0	0.3
N =	430	160	100	110	800

However, when controlling for ethnicity, we find that a majority of the Hmong lack any formal education. Formal education is not an important part of tribal culture and is often unavailable. By comparison, a majority of the Vietnamese and Cambodians have attended at least some high school. The Vietnamese are the only group to have a substantial proportion of refugees with a level of education beyond high school.

Time of arrival is also an important consideration in examining the educational level of refugees. For the purpose of this study, early arrivals included those who entered the United States between 1975 and 1978, and recent arrivals include those who entered after 1978. The latter group is composed largely of boat and land refugees from camps in Thailand and boat people from Vietnam.[5] When controlling for time of arrival, we find that, for the Hmong, 54 percent of the most recent arrivals have no formal education as compared to 20 percent of the early arrivals. For the Lao, 16.8 percent of the recent arrivals have no formal education and none of the early arrivals are without at least an elementary education. Overall, 47 percent of the recent arrivals have no more than an elementary education as compared to 27 percent of the early arrivals.

Size of community. The ability of these refugees to adjust to the American urban environment is dependent on their previous exposure to an urban environment. Urban immigrants can be expected to have an advantage in the resettlement process due to their familiarity with this environment.[6] The size of the Indochinese community from which the head of the household fled is presented by ethnicity in table 5.6. Over 55 percent of these refugees came from communi-

Table 5.6   Home country community size of head of household by ethnicity (in percent)

Community size	Vietnamese	Lao	Hmong	Cambodian	Overall
Less than 500	0.0	1.9	40.0	2.7	5.8
500–1,500	0.2	8.1	21.0	29.1	8.4
1,500–10,000	0.9	8.8	11.0	30.0	7.8
10,000–100,000	11.6	15.6	27.0	18.2	15.3
100,000+	82.6	43.8	0.0	19.1	55.8
Don't know/no answer	4.7	21.9	1.0	0.9	7.1
N =	430	160	100	110	800

ties of 100,000 or more. The Vietnamese and Lao can be classified as urbanites, while the Hmong and Cambodians are more likely to be rural. In comparing early arrivals and recent arrivals, we also find that recent arrivals tend to come from less urbanized environments. However, this difference is not the same for each ethnic group. Among the Cambodians, recent arrivals are slightly more urban than early arrivals.

Prearrival occupations. The occupational status of refugees in their home country varies with ethnicity. In general, respondents are likely to be from a military, professional, or farm labor background.

Our findings, presented in table 5.7, indicate that the Vietnamese are the most likely to be professionals and white collar workers. The

Table 5.7   Home country occupation of head of household (in percent)

	Vietnamese	Lao	Hmong	Cambodian	Overall
Never employed	11.2	0.6	5.0	2.7	7.1
Self employed	5.6	0.0	7.0	7.3	4.9
Professional	11.6	8.8	6.0	2.7	9.1
Managers	4.2	3.8	0.0	0.9	3.1
Merchants	10.0	1.9	0.0	1.8	6.0
Sales workers	1.4	0.6	0.0	12.7	2.6
Clerical	2.8	1.3	0.0	3.6	2.3
Craftsmen	3.5	2.5	1.0	4.5	3.1
Assembly workers	2.8	0.6	0.0	0.9	1.8
Equipment operatives	0.5	3.8	1.0	0.9	1.3
Laborers (nonfarm)	6.3	0.0	0.0	0.9	3.5
Farm laborer	0.9	8.8	6.0	23.6	6.3
Family farm laborer	0.0	0.0	0.0	0.0	0.0
Farmer (own or rent)	0.9	1.9	3.0	3.6	1.8
Migrant workers	0.0	0.0	0.0	0.0	0.0
Service workers	5.8	11.9	1.0	3.6	6.2
Homemakers	3.5	6.3	0.0	2.7	3.5
Military	17.9	34.4	62.0	22.7	27.4
Police	0.2	3.8	3.0	0.0	1.3
Student	9.8	8.8	3.0	3.6	7.0
Other	0.2	0.6	0.0	0.9	0.4
Don't know/no answer	0.9	0.0	2.0	0.0	0.7
N =	430	160	100	110	800

Laotians tend to be professionals, blue collar workers, and soldiers. The majority of the Hmong served in support of United States troops in Laos. Cambodians were evenly split among the military, farm laborers, and sales workers. The military orientation of these groups creates a problem for resettlement. They will need to be retrained for viable positions in an urban society.

Postarrival Conditions

The complexity of the adaptation and assimilation problems are also reflected in the differences in postarrival environments. Some refugees have positive living conditions that encourage self-sufficiency and assimilation. For others, the economic conditions and disparities between prearrival and postarrival conditions can only add to a lengthy adaptation process. The following variables and discussion provide a picture of current refugee living conditions.

Mobility. The phenomenon of secondary migration has widespread reverberations for resettlement policy. In the initial resettlement site, the refugee has a sponsor. In the new location he probably has a relative or family friends. However, initial resettlement of refugees near relatives does not assure that secondary migration will not occur.[7] McInnis has found that the second most frequently cited reason for secondary migration is employment, followed by climate and difficulty with sponsors and communities.[8] On the positive side, secondary migration is a sign of independence. On the negative side, it creates a sense of loss and disillusionment for sponsors and voluntary agencies.

California is one of the states that receive primary and secondary migrants in large numbers. The initial resettlement location for our respondents is presented, by ethnicity, in table 5.8. San Diego was the primary resettlement site for a majority of the refugees in our sample. The Vietnamese have been the most mobile, while the Cambodians have been the least mobile. The Laotians are the most frequent migrants from other cities in California.

Time of arrival is a factor in the high mobility of the Vietnamese refugees, with early arrivals more likely than recent arrivals to have moved to a new location in the United States. Perhaps the extensive networks of Vietnamese community associations and religious

Table 5.8 Initial resettlement location of head of household by ethnicity (in percent)

	Vietnamese	Lao	Hmong	Cambodian	Overall
San Diego	70.5	76.3	86.0	82.7	75.3
California cities other than San Diego	8.1	9.4	4.0	8.2	7.9
States other than California	21.4	14.4	10.0	9.1	16.9
N =	430	160	100	110	800

organizations tend to act as locator services for friends and distant relatives.

Housing. Housing is an important factor in the resettlement of refugees. The larger nuclear and extended families create a special problem for local communities that do not have the quantity and the quality of space that is needed. Further, discrimination by landlords and homeowners has created some problems in finding adequate housing. Although voluntary agencies provide much of the initial support in the location of housing for refugees, there are problems in the availability and quality of housing that is suitable for refugee needs.

Results from the San Diego study reveal that most refugees are renters (see table 5.9), with the Vietnamese among the most likely to own a home. The Cambodians are more likely to be home dwellers, while the Laotians and Hmong are more likely to be apartment dwellers. These differences may be due to some extent to voluntary agency practices of resettling refugees in different areas of the city or to different ethnic groups developing communities in different areas of the city where the housing stock is either house- or apartment-oriented.

Housing mobility is another indicator of the stability of the refugee population in San Diego. Nearly half of the refugee population have lived in their present residence for less than one year (see table 5.10). Another third of the households have been in their current residence for less than two years. The Laotians, who are mainly apartment dwellers, are the most mobile. Problems in adapting to apartment life have been attributed to the size of the family and the consequent noise. The Laotians and the Hmong, who concentrate in

Table 5.9 Current housing of head of household by ethnicity (in percent)

	Vietnamese	Lao	Hmong	Cambodian	Overall
Own home	10.7	0.0	0.0	1.8	6.0
Own other	0.7	1.9	3.0	3.6	1.7
Rent home	46.7	7.5	20.0	75.5	39.5
Rent apartment	39.1	86.9	77.0	19.1	50.6
Rent other	2.8	3.8	0.0	0.0	2.3
N =	430	160	100	110	800

apartment clusters, are late arrivals and are at present experiencing the initial stages of assimilation.

Postarrival income. The monthly household income reported by the head of household in table 5.11 indicates that most refugee households are earning a below-poverty income. The $700 to $1000 per month is the largest income category. Within this income group we find that every ethnic group except the Vietnamese is equally represented.

These findings are deceiving in the absence of a control for household size. Under this control, the larger refugee households are found to have the larger household incomes. Forty percent of the households with incomes between $700 and $1000 have five to seven household members. Forty-seven percent of the households with incomes between $1000 and $1600 have more than seven persons. Thus, household size contributes to income. The higher-income households, because of this, still tend to earn below poverty incomes.

Postarrival occupations. The current occupation of head of household indicates a tendency toward downward mobility among refugees (see table 5.12). About one-third of the currently employed

Table 5.10 Length of residence in current dwelling of head of household by ethnicity (in percent)

	Vietnamese	Lao	Hmong	Cambodian	Overall
Less than 1 year	39.6	50.0	37.0	33.6	40.5
1–2 years	32.1	40.1	41.0	37.3	35.5
2–3 years	16.0	8.1	18.0	23.6	15.8
More than 3 years	12.3	1.9	4.0	5.5	8.3
N =	430	160	100	110	800

Table 5.11   Monthly household income by ethnicity (in percent)

	Vietnamese	Lao	Hmong	Cambodian	Overall
$0–700	21.9	20.0	17.0	29.1	21.9
$700–1,000	29.5	34.4	34.0	34.5	31.8
$1,000–1,300	14.4	21.9	28.0	18.2	18.1
$1,300–1,600	11.4	12.5	15.0	8.2	11.6
$1,600–1,900	6.0	8.8	3.0	7.3	6.4
$1,900+	14.1	1.9	3.0	2.7	8.8
Don't know/no answer	2.6	0.6	0.0	0.0	1.5
N =	430	160	100	110	800

refugees are equipment operatives. This designation includes a number of occupations that are linked to special construction, janitorial, industrial, and electronic equipment. Fewer than 1 percent were equipment operatives prior to their forced migration. A similar disparity is present in the crafts, professional, and public and private service work categories. Apparently, many of those with a military and public service background have made a transition to the occupations that create the least difficulty in terms of employment barriers. In general, there has been a decrease in occupations that require independence and an increase in the type of occupations that were typical of other Asian immigrants.

Conclusion

In general, the basic characteristics of the Indochinese refugee community in San Diego are similar to the refugee population as a whole. When compared to other immigrants, the Indochinese tend to be younger, married, and more likely to be involved in some type of manual labor. Although many of the respondents fled Indochina without all of their family members, there has been a tendency toward reunification. In addition, the tradition of the extended family as an economic unit remains intact.

The findings of this survey reveal a population that is readjusting to a new society. The occupational downward mobility and limited employment opportunities are indicated by high unemployment. The early arriving Vietnamese have made inroads through refugee businesses and the professional sector. However, refugees who have

Table 5.12   Current occupation of head of household by ethnicity
(in percent)

	Vietnamese	Lao	Hmong	Cambodian	Overall
Self employed	0.5	0.0	0.0	0.0	0.3
Professional	21.2	0.0	0.0	0.0	12.9
Managerial	1.6	0.0	0.0	0.0	1.0
Merchant	1.1	0.0	0.0	0.0	0.7
Sales	2.2	0.0	0.0	0.0	1.3
Clerical	6.5	1.8	9.5	4.8	5.9
Crafts	21.2	21.4	19.0	9.5	20.1
Operatives	22.3	51.8	23.8	52.4	30.0
Transportation	3.3	1.8	0.0	4.8	2.6
Laborer	4.3	7.1	2.4	0.0	4.3
Public and private service work	8.2	14.3	38.1	28.6	14.9
Service work	7.1	1.8	7.1	0.0	5.6
Other	0.5	0.0	0.0	0.0	0.3
Total applicable	185	56	42	21	304
Inapplicable (unemployed)	245	104	58	89	496
Total	430	160	100	110	800

recently arrived do not presently have the employment skills necessary for living in a technological society.

A number of potential resettlement problems can be discerned from these basic data. Health, employment, assimilation, education, and language problems are among them. The following chapters address the refugee perceptions and experiences concerning each of these problems.

6
Health
Status
and
Utilization

Refugee populations are extremely vulnerable to disease and illness during their period of migration. The rapidity of the movement prevents the effectiveness of normal health precautions. Furthermore, the conditions of refugee camps in countries of first asylum contribute to the health risks faced by the refugee. Since host societies tend to be ill prepared for the involuntary migrant, they often lack the facilities and resources necessary to remedy many of these unexpected health problems.

When medical help is available, refugees exhibit a wide range of health practices and beliefs. Many Indochinese refugees are from societies in which self-care is determined by local customs and traditions. As a result, they tend to avoid Western medical practices. They lack knowledge of the benefits of these practices, exhibit fears over treatment, and often do not follow up treatment with preventive care. Complicating matters are the problems of language, social habits, and general uncertainty about their own future.

Most refugees arrive in the United States after initial medical screening in the country of first asylum. In many cases the preliminary screening efforts do not detect diseases which are not prevalent in Western societies. American physicians rarely experience cholera, leprosy, malaria, smallpox, or tuberculosis. Among the most recent refugees, the prevalence of certain infectious diseases such as venereal diseases, hepatitis A and B, and intestinal parasites has been well documented. There has also been a prevalence of physical abnormalities and other psychiatric disorders among these refugees.[1]

Thus, the lack of history of medical care makes these refugees different from other immigrants.

The medical screening of refugees is similar to that of other immigrant groups seeking admission to the United States. The screening process begins in refugee camps where medical histories are recorded for each refugee. Language difficulties and a general lack of knowledge prevent an accurate assessment of the refugee's health status. A physical exam often includes only visual inspection, a chest x-ray for persons fifteen years and older, and a blood test for syphilis. Under the Immigration and Nationality Act refugees can be excluded for admission with certain medical conditions. These conditions include leprosy, tuberculosis, and venereal diseases. However, waivers were granted for refugees who have family members in the United States or who were deemed not to present a significant hazard to the American public.

Upon entering a port of entry, the Public Health Service reviews medical histories and performs a perfunctory health examination. Assuming that a detailed medical examination has occurred, the medical records are forwarded to the sponsoring organization, the Center for Disease Control, and state and local health departments. Federal grants are provided for the assessment of health status, but the responsibility for medical treatment and follow-up becomes that of the sponsoring organization.

Criticism tends to emphasize the superficiality of the medical screening process given the impact of refugees on disease rates in various counties. In 1980, Orange County, California, health officials found that the Indochinese refugees had a much higher incidence of contagious diseases than the county native population. For example, tuberculosis incidence rates in Orange County tripled between 1975 and 1980. Similar statistics were found in Seattle, Washington, where 30 percent of the tuberculosis cases were Indochinese refugees. Health officials in Los Angeles and Virginia also experienced a sharp increase in malaria cases, while in Montgomery County, Maryland, 12 percent of the refugees were found to be carriers of hepatitis. In all resettlement sites, parasites were a problem among refugees. Over 72 percent of the refugees examined in Long Beach, California, had this problem. Thus, the quality of the initial screening of refugees has been questioned given the much higher incidence of certain contagious diseases in refugee populations.

It is quite clear that these refugees have serious health problems which significantly affect their resettlement prospects. Present resettlement policy includes a health component, as health status can directly affect other aspects of resettlement such as labor force participation and the demand for public assistance. Besides the observable health problems reflected by local health authorities, migration and resettlement have been shown to have stress-related health effects that may not be present at the initial screening or at the time of arrival.[2] The psychological stress induced by dislocation, family separation, and the loss of homes tends to produce latent symptoms of many social problems that have health consequences.

It is important that the source and effects of psychological stress be identified and managed. Otherwise the longer-term resettlement goals of employment, self-sufficiency, and acculturation cannot be achieved. This chapter identifies these sources by examining the effects of selected psychological and situational aspects of resettlement on the subjective health assessment of the refugees themselves. In addition, it examines the actual health service utilization behaviors of Indochinese refugees. The amount of utilization provides some much-needed information about how well refugees are adapting to the American health care system.

Psychological and Situational Determinants of Health Status

The hazards inherent in the study of subjective health assessments as measures of health status are widely recognized.[3] Implicit in the use of these assessments is the assumption of an accepted normative standard of health. However, objective health and subjective health assessments can be very different, as the latter tends to reflect the norms of a relevant reference group and to change according to psychological states.[4] Nevertheless, previous studies do suggest a relationship among subjective health assessments, physicians' ratings of health, and health service utilization.[5] They have also identified nonmorbidity predictors of subjective health assessments such as psychological states, life satisfaction, and general well-being.[6] In studies of four diverse populations, Tessler and Mechanic identified psychological distress as a consistent predictor of subjective health assessments and Maddox found that subjective health assessments were less positive among persons with a history of depression or low morale.[7] In a national sample, Campbell found that people who were dissatisfied with their health did not have a strong sense of well-being.[8] Thus, even though subjective health assessments must be considered as global interpretations rather than specific reflections of objective health, they do provide a useful measure of the health service needs and health perceptions of a population.

Studies that focus on immigrant and migrant populations have shown that dislocation produces the type of distress that has been associated with reduced subjective health assessments and that a variety of somatic problems attend or follow difficulties in adaptation.[9] Hull, for example, suggests that health changes parallel cultural changes.[10] The difference between the old life and the new life creates "status ambiguity" which increases the risk of illness.

Given these findings, we want to examine the effects that various psychological and situational aspects of resettlement have on the subjective health assessments of Indochinese refugees. The examination will indicate which aspects are the most stress-producing and how these aspects compare with illness in terms of their effect on subjective health assessments. The comparative evaluation is accomplished by controlling for illness when measuring the effects of psychological and situational variables.[11]

A Preliminary Analysis of Subjective Health Assessment

Subjective health assessment was measured by asking respondents to assess their health status on a four-point scale, from "poor" to "excellent." Illness was measured by asking the question "Are you currently being treated by a doctor for any medical problem?" The former question is a widely accepted measure of subjective health status. The latter is not as widely accepted as a measure of illness because it assumes a perfect relationship between illness and health service utilization. Unfortunately, a more accurate measure based on direct physician assessment of health was not available with these data. However, in defense of the use of treatment as a measure of illness, it should be pointed out that health service access is publicly supported through a number of local resettlement programs, including medical assistance programs, health education programs, and medical translation programs. Thus, treatment should be considered a valid, if less than complete, measure of illness.

Table 6.1 Regression analysis of subjective health assessment on morbidity and selected nonmorbidity variables

	Overall	
	Beta	B
ILLNESS	.35	.68
PSYCHOLOGICAL VARIABLES		
Understanding American way of life		
Separation from family		
Lack Indochinese support group	.11	.10
Difficulty dealing with American agencies	.13	.12
SITUATIONAL VARIABLES		
Lack of job skills training programs		
Poor housing		
Transportation		
Year of arrival		
Write English	−.14	−.21
Number of San Diego relatives		
Household size		
Age	−.15	−.01
Marital status		
Income	.08	.04
Employment		
CONTRIBUTION TO R^2		
Illness	.16	
Psychological and situational factors	.12	
Total R^2	.28	

a. Early arrivals are those who arrived between 1975 and 1977.

Early arrivals[a]		Recent arrivals[b]		Vietnamese		Lao		Hmong		Cambodian	
Beta	B	Beta	B	Beta	B	Beta	B	Beta	B	Beta	B
.40	.83	.32	.56	.35	.63	.53	1.4	.45	1.7	.18	.26
				−.11	−.10			.20	.52		
.10	.10	.15	.12	.15	.13						
.16	.15	.13	.12	.22	.20						
										−.26	−.28
						.15	.14	.24	.30		
−.18	−.30									−.37	−.57
−.10	−7.7	−.23	−.02	−.17	−.01	−.20	−.02				
		.14	.08			.18	.12				
				−.13	−.17						
.18		.13		.18		.36		.23		.02	
.12		.11		.17		.09		.10		.18	
.30		.24		.35		.45		.33		.22	

Recent arrivals are those who arrived between 1978 and 1981.

The distress produced by psychological aspects of resettlement was measured by a series of questions in which respondents were asked to rank, on a three-point scale ranging from "very serious" to "not very serious," the problems associated with nine different aspects of resettlement. These aspects were discussed in chapter 5; they include understanding the American way of life, separation of family members, lack of ethnic support groups, housing conditions, transportation, dealing with American agencies, and availability of job skills training programs.

Eight situational variables are included in the model: age, ethnicity, English language ability, number of San Diego relatives, household size, marital status, employment status, and income. These variables are measures of the social support and social skills utilized in coping with the demands of resettlement. It is assumed that these variables will affect the ability of refugees to cope with resettlement demands.

In order to explore the relative explanatory power of these predictors, a multivariate regression model was utilized. The results of the regression analysis for the entire sample as well as separately for early arrivals, recent arrivals, and each ethnic group are given in table 6.1. Both standardized and unstandardized coefficients are used so that comparisons within and between groups can be made.

Overall, illness (as measured by current treatment) explains approximately 16 percent of the variance on subjective health assessments. This proportion does not vary with length of residence, but does vary with ethnicity. Subjective health assessments are more closely associated with illness for the Lao (36 percent of variance explained) and less closely associated with illness for the Cambodian (2 percent variance explained).

The selected psychological and situational variables of resettlement do have an effect on subjective health assessments after the effect of illness has been removed. These variables explain from an additional 9 percent (for the Lao) to an additional 25 percent (for the Cambodians) of the variance in subjective health assessments. Overall, they explain an additional 13 percent of the variance.

The psychological variables with the greatest overall effects on health assessment are measures of adjustment. Problems that are related to interactions with American agencies and problems related to the lack of ethnic support groups show a strong relationship with subjective health assessment. As suggested by Hull and others, the status ambiguity of refugees is fostered by interactions with American resettlement agencies. In addition, Cobb's observation that stress is greater among those whose culture of origin is most different from that of the host community may be a factor with these refugees. Further, the "stress-buffering" role of social support may have been undermined by previous resettlement policies that emphasized dispersal.[12] However, in contrast to our findings, Starr found that the psychological status of those refugees who live in ethnic enclaves differs little from those residing elsewhere.[13]

In sum, unlike previous studies of perceived health status, our study shows that the situational context of the Indochinese does not have a significant effect on their subjective assessment of their health. The situational variables with the greatest effects are level of English language skill and age. The effects of these four variables are similar among recent and early arrivals, indicating that the distress associated with the resettlement experience is not being reduced by length of residence. Especially notable here is the lack of consistency and magnitude of the effects of income and employment. Income has an effect for recent arrivals, and employment had no effect except when controlling for ethnicity. Moreover, we do not find any significant effects when examining the rest of the demographic variables.

Health Service Utilization Patterns

One of the major resettlement problems that Indochinese refugees face is unmet health needs resulting from inadequate health service access and utilization. This problem does not occur during the period of initial resettlement, as newly arrived refugees are routinely screened and treated for a number of acute health problems. However, after initial resettlement, the burden of access and utilization transfers to the refugee and unmet health needs increase.

While financial assistance may guarantee that health services are available to refugees, research on other immigrant populations indicates that effective health service access and utilization require additional forms of assistance that are informational, psychological, and organizational.[14] Accordingly, the models used to study utilization among immigrant populations can be described as sets of situational and attitudinal factors that act as potential barriers to health service utilization.[15] Attitudinal factors include attitudes that might serve as determinants of health behaviors, e.g., perceived health status, acculturation, etc., and situational factors include cultural and financial conditions that might prevent health service access, e.g., employment status, language skill, length of residence, etc.[16] Each type of factor has been found to be useful in predicting utilization, and each has a distinct prescription for health policies regarding Indochinese refugees. Attitudinal factors emphasize the importance of health service delivery policies, and situational factors emphasize the importance of policies in areas other than health, e.g., welfare, education, housing, etc.

Studies based on these models have produced a variety of interesting results. For example, the integration of immigrants into ethnic subcommunities has been cited as one determinant of low health service utilization, and reliance on folk medicines has been proposed as another.[17] Tung found that traditional beliefs and superstitions are among the more common utilization barriers for Indochinese refugees.[18] To the extent that health service utilization of refugees can be compared to that of the urban poor, Indochinese refugees can be expected to delay seeking health care until their health condition has become critical.[19] Although lack of education is also a commonly cited utilization barrier, Welch found that education is not related to utilization among the most recently arrived immigrants.[20] Members of this group tend to get better care when informed of local health services and procedures, regardless of their educational background.

Utilization Behaviors

There is very little data that focuses on the patterns of health service utilization among Indochinese refugees. There is even less data that includes the attitudinal and situational components needed to test the extension of the above results to Indochinese refugees. The purpose of this section is to provide some of this data. It examines the patterns of health service utilization among Indochinese refugees, and it examines the predictors of utilization. A number of attitudinal and situational factors are included in a multivariate analysis of utilization. The results of this analysis are compared with those found in utilization studies of other immigrant populations.

The measures used in this study are consistent with those used in other studies of health service utilization. Utilization measures include both physician and hospital contact and are divided into the two dimensions of contact and volume. Contact measures the achievement of entry into the system, and volume measures the utilization of service after entry.[21] Physician contact is indicated by at least one physician visit during the last three months, and hospital contact is indicated by at least one hospital admission since arrival in the United States. Volume is indicated, in both cases, by the number of contacts that occurred during the period considered.

The health service utilization behavior of Indochinese refugees is presented by length of residence and ethnicity in table 6.2. Overall, 16.6 percent of the refugees have been admitted to a hospital since arrival, and 45.1 percent have seen a physician on an outpatient basis within the last three months. In both cases, there are contact differences associated with length of residence and ethnicity. Hospital contact for early arrivals is more than five times what it is for recent arrivals, and the Lao and Hmong have lower levels of contact than the Vietnamese and Cambodians. Physician contact for Lao is nearly four times what it is for Hmong, and physician contact for recent arrivals is more than fifty percentage points higher than it is for early arrivals.

Inadequate samples make it impossible to determine whether volume of hospital utilization is related to length of residence. It is related to ethnicity. The Lao and Cambodians are high-volume users, and the Hmong are low-volume users. Overall, the percentage of

Table 6.2 Health service utilization by length of residence and ethnicity

Utilization	Length of residence (years)						Viet-namese	Lao	Hmong	Cam-bodian	Total
	1	2	3	4	5	6					
Hospital contact (percent admitted)	4.0	11.3	18.0	23.3	16.7	23.2	19.8	9.4	5.0	24.8	16.6
Hospital volume											
Low volume	0.0	71.0	48.0	50.0	100.0	40.5	56.5	36.8	62.5	39.4	50.7
High volume	100.0	29.0	52.0	50.0	0.0	59.5	43.5	63.2	37.5	60.6	49.3
Physician contact within last 3 mos.	81.1	51.2	41.8	43.7	41.4	26.7	45.5	61.1	14.4	47.5	45.1
Physician volume											
Low volume	38.3	45.4	50.5	63.2	80.0	75.0	61.9	37.5	64.3	35.4	51.7
High volume	61.7	54.6	49.5	36.8	20.0	25.0	38.1	62.5	35.7	64.6	48.3
Total	75	213	239	90	12	168	429	159	100	109	797

high-volume physician utilization does decrease with length of residence. However, this is not the case for the Lao and the Cambodians. Their high volume rates are nearly double the rates for the other two ethnic groups.

There are a number of possible explanations for the length-of-residence and ethnic differences in contact and volume of utilization. Prearrival differences in health behavior, lengths of stay in unsanitary resettlement camps, a program of extensive screening and treatment at the time of arrival, and differences in morbidity are among them. The length-of-residence increase in hospital contact may also be due to the fact that early arrivals have been here longer and are more likely to have developed a medical problem requiring hospitalization.

The relationships between length of residence, ethnicity, and perceived health status are given in table 6.3. The percentage of refugees who consider themselves to be in excellent health ranges from fewer than 19 percent among the most recent arrivals to more than 40 percent among the early arrivals. The initially low perception and subsequent improvement in perceived health status provides further evidence that refugees arrive with health problems that improve after initial treatment.

The Lao are the most likely to consider themselves in excellent health, and the Hmong are among the most likely to consider their health status no better than fair. This suggests different perceptions concerning the importance of health service facilities in providing treatment for health problems, for the Lao have high rates of physician contact and the Hmong have low rates of both physician and hospital contact.

Table 6.3   Perceived health status by length of residence and ethnicity

Perceived health status	Length of residence (years)						Viet-namese	Lao	Hmong	Cam-bodian	Total
	1	2	3	4	5	6					
Poor	1.3	2.8	5.0	6.7	0.0	1.8	3.3	3.8	5.0	2.7	3.5
Fair	18.7	20.9	15.8	17.8	16.7	12.5	13.5	16.9	23.0	25.5	17.0
Good	61.3	52.1	51.3	42.2	58.3	42.8	52.1	40.6	44.0	59.1	49.8
Excellent	18.7	23.3	27.5	32.2	25.0	42.3	31.2	38.8	23.0	12.7	29.1
Total	75	213	239	89	12	167	430	160	95	110	795

Predictors of Utilization Behaviors

The above description of utilization behaviors provides basic but badly needed data on the health service utilization of Indochinese refugees. However, it falls short of addressing more complicated questions concerning the combined effects of situational and attitudinal factors on utilization patterns. A multivariate regression model is more appropriate for addressing these questions, and it allows for the identification of the relative importance of each variable for comparisons of contact and volume variables, and for assessments of the combined effects of the situational and attitudinal variables in explaining refugee utilization of health services. The order of entry of the predictor variables in the regression equation is governed by their proximity to the refugee's current situation. Thus, the attitudinal variables are entered first, ethnicity is entered last, and the remaining situational variables are allowed to enter in the order of their contribution to the explained variance in the utilization variables. The hierarchical model is used to manage the interaction between proximate variables (such as level of English communication skills) and distant variables (such as ethnicity). If the distant variables were allowed to enter first, they could mask effects that are more appropriately attributed to proximate variables.

The regression analyses and standardized regression coefficients for the hospital and physician contact and volume models are given in table 6.4. The magnitudes of the R^2s in these equations range from .12 for hospital contact to .27 for physician contact. Though much of the variance in contact and volume is left unexplained by the equations, the situational and attitudinal factors that do contribute to the explained variance are noteworthy because their patterns of relative contribution vary from those found in more general studies.[22]

The effect of length of residence on utilization behavior is not diminished when the effects of other independent variables are simultaneously considered. Refugees who have been in the United States longer are more likely than recently arrived refugees to have been admitted to a hospital since arrival, but less likely to have had physician contact within the last three months.

Consistent with previous findings, ethnicity is also an important factor in the regression models, with Hmong refugees appearing as low utilizers in three of the four utilization categories. Vietnamese,

Table 6.4 Regression analysis for situational and attitudinal variables associated with health utilization measures

Predictors	Hospital contact	Hospital volume	Physician contact	Physician volume
SITUATIONAL VARIABLES				
Length of residence	+.22		−.06	−.18
Household size		−.13		
Age		+.29		
Married	+.11			
Male	−.09	−.15	−.07	
Education				
Home country	−.10		+.06	
United States	+.07		−.05	
Ethnicity				
Vietnamese			−.08	−.22
Lao	−.08			−.15
Hmong	−.18		−.30	−.15
Cambodian			−.16	
Religion (Western)				
English				
Read	−.05			−.07
Write				
Income	+.06	−.26	−.05	
Employed	−.09		−.08	
Medical assistance			+.10	−.12
ATTITUDINAL VARIABLES				
Perceived health status	−.16	+.15	−.29	−.20
Acculturation	+.05	+.22	+.02	
Perceived self-sufficiency			+.08	+.04
R^2	.12	.24	.27	.16

Note: All coefficients are Betas and $p < .05$ for each entry.

although among the most likely to have utilized these services, are not high-volume users. It is plausible that the Vietnamese have less severe health problems because they are more likely to seek early treatment for the problems due to their prearrival familiarity with health service attributed to related differences in perceiving health status. Likewise, ethnic differences in utilization cannot be attributed to the fact that refugees from one ethnic group have generally been here longer than refugees from another ethnic group. The regression analysis indicates major ethnic differences in health behavior and utilization. It also indicates a more lengthy socialization period with regard to the utilization of health services.

Conclusions

Although these findings are based on a restricted sample of Indochinese refugees, their implications are useful in evaluating substantive policy issues concerning the health care needs of these refugees and in assessing the need for future research in this area. The limited utilization of health services by the Hmong can perhaps be improved by a more comprehensive effort at health promotion and by targeted efforts to improve health service delivery to this group. The very fact that utilization among this group is low further suggests that cultural differences may act as a barrier to the perception of illness and the utilization of health services even when those services are subsidized. Encounters with health service providers may imply a threatened punishment or deprivation given the refugees' previous experiences. It may also imply failure in the face of impossible behavioral demands.[23]

Finally, adequate health care begins with health perceptions. It is important to begin to study the perception of health and illness from the viewpoint of the refugee. In-depth analysis of the cultural dimensions of health perceptions and behaviors would help in understanding the uniqueness of present adjustment problems. These disparate cultural influences affect inclinations toward the use of services and create unmet needs. A health policy that promotes socialization to the health care system could reduce that problem in present resettlement programs.

7
Education and Language

The acquisition of English language communication skills has long been recognized as a dominant factor in the successful assimilation and resettlement of refugees.[1] English is required for social intercourse and is central to the acquisition of necessities such as food, clothing, shelter, and transportation. Immigrants to the United States have not always been provided with specialized education and training in the use of the English language. However, since 1914, government-sponsored programs for English language training have been implemented for the purpose of accelerating the Americanization of immigrants. State legislatures have passed laws and allocated funds for adult education classes that provide immigrant language training. The acquisition of English language skills has since become associated with the acquisition of American values and the minimization of ethnic values.[2]

At present there are few empirical studies that focus on English language literacy or the acquisition of English language communication skills among Indochinese refugees. This chapter focuses on refugee literacy levels and the utilization of language training services. It also investigates the relationship between language training and employment.

English through ESL

The problem of instructing Indochinese refugees in the use of English is directly related to the fact that they speak languages that are rarely spoken and even more rarely studied in Western countries. Although these refugees do receive basic "survival" English instruction in refugee camps, this instruction is limited to basic vocabulary. It provides few of the skills needed to reach language fluency.[3] Upon arrival, all refugees are urged to study English through ESL courses.

The ESL movement represents a departure from the standard methodologies of teaching English.[4] The methodology and drills, which draw on newer findings in linguistics and psychology, tend to be more meaningful and less mechanical. Further, the approach emphasizes the utility of vocabulary items and the social context of their use.

ESL programs are funded by city, county, state, federal, and voluntary agencies.[5] The usual setting for an ESL program is an adult evening school or a postsecondary institution. Voluntary agencies also hold classes in churches, labor union facilities, storefronts, and industrial sites. The diversity of providers and locations has made it difficult for the development of a single governmental policy concerning the standards and aims of ESL in the resettlement process.[6]

The importance of ESL in the resettlement of refugees in California is indicated by mandatory attendance for all able-bodied welfare recipients. Each welfare recipient is required to attend one three-hour ESL session per day for a week. In San Diego, six adult learning centers and several private and voluntary agencies supply San Diego with ESL training. At the present time, most of these services are funded by the State of California. Refugees may enroll in ESL or Vocational English as a Second Language (VESL), but not both.

The typical ESL program includes a number of different classes, including orientation to English, beginning English, general English, prevocational English, and advanced English.[7] In most cases, ESL students are placed in one of the various levels of classes according to the results of a brief oral interview. Refugees are permitted to move through the different levels according to an individual assessment of their abilities. Bilingual aides are available to assist most refugees in the acquisition of English language skills. However, classes are not segregated by ethnicity or refugee status. Thus, classes are typically composed of European as well as Indochinese refugees.

The programs are generally set up to provide at least one year of English language training. The original goal was to provide three years of language training. Unfortunately, the eighteen-month limitation on assistance from federally reimbursed funds has resulted in a lowering of attendance rates and a shift from daytime classes to evening classes. At present, the effects on private voluntary efforts have not been determined, but similar experiences are expected.

The curricula of ESL programs grew out of a need to focus on advanced level native language speakers. The text materials were developed on two levels.[8] First, primarily oral materials were developed to deal with survival and employment needs. Second, additional materials were developed around real-life situations and tasks that a refugee must perform in social settings. The emphasis of these latter materials is not linguistic competence, but social competence.

Each of the language curricula focuses on a specific social situation. For example, the general vocational curriculum focuses on the language skills necessary for getting and keeping a job. The literacy curriculum focuses on literacy for the nonliterate or semiliterate second language learners. And the home management ESL curriculum focuses on the skills needed to run a household in the United States. New curricula are constantly being devised and revised to foster retention and growth in language skills. Unfortunately, these curricula have not been sufficient to surmount the language problems that these refugees face. The seriousness of the problem is indicated in table 7.1. In San Diego, almost three-fourths of the refugees interviewed perceive English language communication to be a very serious problem for themselves and their community. The Hmong experience the most difficulty and the Vietnamese experience the least difficulty. Hmong tribesmen have special linguistic problems, such as the absence of a written native language, which prevent easy acquisition of a second language. Many of the Vietnamese, on the other hand, have English language experience due to their proximity to U.S. military forces in Vietnam. The Laotians and Cambodians experience problems similar to those of the Hmong, but not to the same degree.

Table 7.1 Perception of English language problem by ethnicity (in percent)

	Vietnamese	Lao	Hmong	Cambodian	Overall
Very serious	65.8	82.5	95.0	73.6	73.9
Somewhat serious	16.5	12.5	4.0	19.1	14.5
Not very serious	17.2	4.4	1.0	7.3	11.3
Total	430	160	100	110	800

On the positive side, the impact of ESL programs is evident in comparisons between the problems of early arrivals and recent arrivals. While 73 percent of the most recently arrived refugees mention English language as a serious problem, only 55 percent of the early arrivals mention it as a serious problem. There is some improvement despite the continued high proportion of refugees who mention language as a problem after a lengthy U.S. residency.

Literacy

The acquisition of language skills includes the ability to read and write as well as speak. These skills are not only necessary for assimilation, they are highly correlated with refugee self-sufficiency.[9] Unfortunately the task of achieving English language literacy is sometimes compounded by refugees' illiteracy in their native tongue.

Literacy in both the English language and the respondent's native language was measured by a two-part question. The first part focuses on the ability to read an English or native language newspaper and the second focuses on the ability to complete a job application in English or the native language. Clearly, the focus of the question is on survival-level literacy. The distribution of responses on this question is given in table 7.2. Fifty-six percent of the refugees report that they are unable to perform either task in English. However, the majority of refugees do not have a literacy problem in their native language: 85.6 percent report native language literacy.

Table 7.2   Level of literacy (in percent)

| Language | Overall | Ethnicity | | | | Arrival | |
		Vietnamese	Lao	Hmong	Cambodian	Early	Recent
ENGLISH							
able to read and write	44.0	52.6	42.8	31.0	24.5	68.4	31.6
unable to read and write	56.0	47.4	57.2	69.0	75.5	31.6	68.4
NATIVE LANGUAGE							
able to read and write	85.6	93.0	91.3	54.0	77.3	93.7	81.5
unable to read and write	14.4	7.0	8.8	46.0	22.7	6.3	18.5

The differences in literacy between ethnic groups are quite pronounced. Vietnamese are twice as likely as Cambodians to be literate in English. About one-fourth (24.5 percent) of the Cambodians are literate, about one-third (31.0 percent) of the Hmong are literate, and fewer than one half (42.8 percent) of the Laotians are literate. The Vietnamese are also the most likely to be literate in their native language, followed closely by Laotians. Although the Hmong are more likely to report English literacy than Cambodians, the Hmong are less likely than the Cambodians to be able to read and write in their own language.

Literacy Predictors

Table 7.3 lists, in descending order, the correlations between literacy in English and a number of independent variables. The list includes three measures of education: education in the refugee's home country, education since coming to the United States, and the combined educational achievement in both the refugee's home country and the United States.

Combined education proves to be the best predictor of literacy in English. The correlation between combined education and English language literacy is .559. Thus, 31 percent of the variance in English language literacy is explained by combined educational achievement. Although native language literacy does not predict literacy in English as well as does education, the correlation between native and English language literacy is still moderately high (.336).

While native language literacy and education in home country are both related to literacy in English, they are related to one another as well. Thus, in an effort to improve our prediction of English lan-

Table 7.3 Correlation analysis of English literacy

Total education (combined home country and United States)	.559
Home country education	.544
U.S. education	.475
Native language literacy	.336
Length of U.S. residence	.326
ESL attendance (past vs. current)	.348
Months of past ESL attendance	−.076
Months of current ESL attendance	.043

guage literacy, we created an additional variable combining both home country education and literacy in native language. Those who had neither formal education nor literacy in their native language were ranked the lowest on this new education-literacy scale. Those who had some education but who had not achieved native language literacy were ranked second lowest, and those who had achieved native language literacy in spite of a lack of formal education were third lowest. The remaining literate respondents were rank-ordered on this scale above the others in ascending order of their home country educational achievement.

We found this education-native literacy scale to be more strongly related to English language literacy than is native language literacy alone. However, it is no more strongly related to English language literacy than are the single and combined measures of education. Thus, the explanatory value of education is not improved by adding a native language literacy component.

Length of residence in the United States also correlates moderately with English language literacy ($r = .326$). This is not surprising for two reasons. First, refugees who have lived in the United States for a longer period have had more time to learn English. Second, the earlier arrivals were better educated than the more recent arrivals. However, a comparison of the English abilities of early and recent arrivals at each educational level reveals that length of residence does have some effect on English language literacy independent of the effects of home country education. The impact of ESL on literacy is complex, given the dynamics of ESL experiences. Although a comparison between those who have attended versus those who have never attended ESL classes reveals a negative relationship between attendance and English literacy, those who are currently enrolled in ESL are presumably enrolled because they have not yet become literate. The negative relationship should not be surprising.

A second way of examining the relationship between ESL attendance and literacy is to dichotomize ESL attendance into those who attended in the past and those who are currently attending or who never attended. When ESL attendance is dichotomized this way, it explains less than 6 percent of the variance in English language literacy. Even if the measure excludes those who have never attended and focuses only on the differences between those who attended in the past and those who are currently attending, we find that ESL attendance explains only 12 percent of the variance in English language literacy.

Refugees who attended in the past were apparently aided by ESL training, as their level of literacy is higher than it is among those who are currently attending. However, length of ESL attendance (either current or past) is not significantly related to literacy in English. Because ESL students begin classes with such widely divergent levels of proficiency, the lack of relationship between length of ESL attendance and literacy in English is not surprising.

Theoretical studies suggest several social factors that may influence the rate of successful second language learning. The ideal language learning environment is described as one in which (1) the group that is learning the second language is nondominant in its environment; (2) the group that is learning intends to remain in the area for an extended period; (3) the group that is learning is small and noncohesive; (4) the target language and learning group cultures are congruent; and (5) both the target and learning groups desire assimilation and have positive attitudes toward each other. The greater the social distance between these groups, the more difficult learning becomes for the learning group.[10]

Mere exposure to the target language, however, is insufficient for acquisition. In theories of second language learning, acquisition is defined as "the process of developing language competence in predictable stages without formal instruction but through active involvement with the target language."[11] It requires a high degree of contact with the target language and exploitation of practice opportunities. The ability to learn a second language, on the other hand, is highly dependent upon the prior learning experiences that educated adults can rely upon.

Studies show that, among educated adults,

> formal instruction is in general of more benefit for SLL [second language learning] than is exposure to the use of the second language in natural situations. . . . A strong correlation was found between years of formal study of English and English proficiency, but only a weak relationship existed between the number of years the student lived in an English-speaking country and proficiency in English.[12]

The following model illustrates and tests the effects of acquisition and learning variables on the achievement of English language literacy among the Indochinese refugees in our sample. It is designed to measure the direct and indirect effects of the independent variables and to sort out their relative weights. Acquisition is dependent upon involvement with the target language and is operationalized as years of residence in the United States, while learning is dependent upon years of formal education and is measured as such. Native language literacy is also included in the model as a supplementary measure of formal language knowledge.

Home country education is chronologically the first independent variable. Education influences native language literacy which in turn influences English language literacy. Home country education also directly influences English language literacy. Thus, our model takes the form shown in figure 7.1.

A regression analysis based on this model produces an R^2 of .374. Together, the three variables account for more than 37 percent of the variance in English language literacy. The coefficients shown on each path of the model are the beta weights from the regression of each dependent variable on the independent variable(s). Home country education has the greatest influence on English language literacy. In addition to its direct effect on English language literacy (.408), it

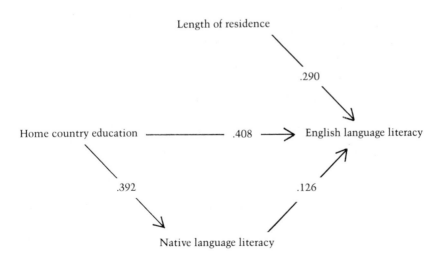

has an indirect effect through its influence on native language literacy. The total direct and indirect influence of home country education on English literacy is represented by a beta weight of .457.

The model demonstrates that length of residence in the United States and native language literacy have moderate influences on English language literacy independent of the effect of education. Thus, those who are achieving literacy in English are influenced more significantly by previous education than by length of U.S. residence.

Previous education is one factor which attenuates the problems of educators in implementing ESL training strategies. Both teaching theories and practice rely upon assumptions that are unmet in the case of Indochinese refugees. Among the refugees who have had previous exposure to and active involvement with Americans and Western culture, reliance on formal education in acquiring English proficiency need not be great. Yet it is precisely this group which has both resided in this country for the longest periods and has obtained the highest levels of education. Conversely, those who have had the least previous exposure to and the least current contact with Americans and the American way of life are also the least educated. Table 7.4 shows that there is a substantial number of people who could be affected by this problem.

Approximately 40 percent of those sampled have little or no formal education. The Hmong are the least educated, and the Vietnamese are the most highly educated. Over half of the Laotians have little or no formal education, while the same percentage of Cambodians have had some high school education. Of the Vietnamese, almost 40 percent have attended trade school, are high school graduates, or are college-educated. Sixteen percent of the Laotians fill

Table 7.4 Education by ethnicity and year of arrival (in percent)

Language	Ethnicity				Arrival	
	Vietnamese	Lao	Hmong	Cambodian	Early	Recent
No formal/elementary	26.4	52.5	81.0	43.6	28.0	47.4
Some high school	33.6	31.3	18.0	52.7	34.0	33.8
High school or trade school graduate	12.1	11.9	1.0	2.7	11.6	8.3
Beyond high school	27.8	4.4	0.0	0.9	26.5	10.6
N =	428	160	100	110	268	530

these same categories, while only about 4 percent of the Cambodians and 1 percent of the Hmong have attained any of these levels.

Comparing the early and more recently arrived refugees, the
greatest differences in educational levels exist within the lowest and
highest categories. While over one-fourth of those who entered this
country before 1979 had some elementary or no formal education,
almost one half of those who were admitted after 1978 have little or
no formal education. The number of refugees entering with more
than a high school education has dropped by about 16 percent.

Table 7.5 provides data on English language literacy levels within
each education category for those who have attended ESL in the past
and are not currently enrolled. This group represents approximately
one-fourth of the total refugee sample. The median number of months
in ESL among this group decreases as educational level increases. It
ranges from 11.5 months for those with the least education to 4.8
months for those at the highest levels of education.

Although this table does not provide an explanation, it is interesting to note that the ESL dropout rate among students who have not
attained proficiency in English increases as their educational level
decreases. Nearly 97 percent of those with an education beyond the
high school level could read and write English after attending ESL.
Although this group may have had some English language skills before
enrolling in ESL, it would seem reasonable to expect the less educated to also emerge from the courses with at least enough knowledge to read an English newspaper and fill out a job application in
English. Indeed, over three-quarters of those with a high school
diploma or trade school experience are capable of doing so, as are
about two-thirds of those with some high school experience. However, among those with little or no formal education, almost 79

Table 7.5 English language literacy among those who have attended ESL
classes in the past (in percent)

English literacy	Education			
	No formal elementary	Some high school	High school or trade graduate	Beyond high school
Able to read and write	21.1	62.6	79.2	97.6
Unable to read and write	78.9	37.4	20.8	2.4
N =	38	91	24	41

Table 7.6   English as a second language by employment status of head of household (in percent)

	Past attendance	Presently attending	Never attended	Overall
Employed	74.4	14.8	60.3	38.0
Unemployed	12.3	28.5	4.4	20.3
Not seeking employment	13.3	52.7	33.1	39.0
N =	195	452	136	800

percent did not obtain these survival level skills before dropping out of ESL.

While the traditional ESL classroom environment may work well for those with formal educational experience, it is not surprising that the

> adults enrolled in intensive ESL programs at universities would outperform nonacademically oriented foreign adults, and especially those with little or no formal education. Second language learners with limited formal education in their first language simply do not have the experience or skills necessary to formalize language data into rules to which they can refer.[13]

ESL, Literacy, and Employment

While the following chapter focuses in detail on a wide range of labor force participation and employment status determinants, it does not

Table 7.7   Employment status by English as a second language by year of arrival (in percent)

		Early Arrivals	
		Attended ESL in past	Currently attending
	Employed	75.9	44.3
	Unemployed	9.3	27.1
	Not seeking employment	14.8	22.9
	N =	108	70

provide an extensive analysis of the employment effects of ESL attendance and English language literacy. We provide this analysis in this
chapter as a preliminary assessment of the importance of these two
variables in the assimilation process.

Table 7.6 indicates a strong relationship between ESL attendance
and employment status. Those who have finished attending ESL are
employed (74.4 percent) and those who are currently attending are
either unemployed (28.5 percent) or not seeking employment (52.7
percent). Those who have never attended are similar to those who
have finished, but have a lower labor force participation rate (66.9
percent versus 86.7 percent).

When length of residence is considered, there is a change in the
relationship between those who have finished ESL and those who
have never attended (see table 7.7). Among early arrivals, those who
have never attended are barely distinguishable from those who have
finished. Among recent arrivals, those who have never attended are
much closer to those who are currently attending. In the first instance,
those who never attended are employed (79.8 percent). In the second,
they tend not to be in the labor force (61.5 percent). This may be due
to the relationship between length of residence and prearrival exposure to English. Early arrivals who have not attended ESL were literate
when they arrived. Recent arrivals who have not attended ESL are not
interested in or not able to seek employment so have not pursued ESL.

Given the requirement that able-bodied refugees who are receiving public assistance must enroll in an ESL class, the relationship
between employment and ESL could be considered spurious. However, the implications of tables 7.6 and 7.7 are reinforced in table 7.8. It

Never Attended ESL	Recent Arrivals			Overall	
	Attended ESL in past	Currently attending	Never attended ESL	Early arrivals	Recent arrivals
79.8	72.4	9.4	28.8	68.9	22.3
3.6	16.1	28.8	5.8	12.2	24.3
15.5	11.5	58.1	61.5	17.0	50.2
84	87	382	52	270	530

Table 7.8   Literacy by employment status of head of household (in percent)

	Write	Do not write	Overall	Read	Do not read	Overall
Employed	60.9	15.2	38.0	61.7	18.3	38.0
Unemployed	17.3	23.2	20.3	18.2	22.0	20.3
Not seeking employment	19.3	58.6	39.0	17.6	56.8	39.0
N =	399	401	800	363	437	800

describes the relationship between English language literacy and employment status. Those who can write tend to be employed (60.9 percent) and those who do not write tend not even to be seeking employment (58.6 percent). Similarly, those who can read tend to be employed (61.7 percent) and those who do not read tend not even to be seeking employment (56.8 percent). There is no doubt, based on these three tables, that English language literacy is a crucial component of the employment process and that the completion of an ESL course provides an opportunity to attain literacy.

Conclusions

English language training is an important and vital service to all Indochinese refugees who are unskilled in English language communication. This service is not an isolated or independent facet of resettlement. On the contrary, training in English serves to facilitate acculturation and self-sufficiency. It is important to recognize, however, that the language training needs of different refugee groups may be quite different and that to apply the same language training techniques to the educated and uneducated may be a mistake.

Theories concerning second language acquisition and learning suggest that second language learning is highly dependent upon prior learning experience. In light of the fact that many Indochinese refugees have little or no formal education, we suggest that a closer examination of the process of language acquisition would be a useful target for further research. Language acquisition is dependent upon high involvement with the target language, yet we know that refugees with the least education are the least likely to be involved with

English outside of the ESL classroom. As ESL is not designed to raise the general educational level of refugees, it may prove beneficial for those with little formal education to be in a classroom environment that incorporates our most current knowledge about the language acquisition process.

8
Employment

Although the issues discussed in previous chapters are all central to the resettlement effort, self-sufficiency and employment are certainly the most frequently cited issues in evaluations of the U.S. resettlement effort. Refugees cannot be considered to be successfully resettled if they require social support and they cannot be free of social support without employment. Employment and self-sufficiency are particularly troublesome issues for Indochinese refugees, as they did not come to the United States to market skills that are supported by the U.S. economy. They came to escape persecution, and they came with few of the skills that are supported by the economy. Deficiencies in English language communication skills, education, and job skills render many Indochinese refugees noncompetitive. Indeed, refugee resettlement policies have assumed that a short-term need for public assistance is unavoidable and have focused on the reduction of an anticipated long-term need that might exist if refugees did not obtain marketable skills. The three years of specialized public assistance that were provided by the Refugee Act of 1980 were designed to facilitate the development of such skills.

For the purpose of this analysis, the employment process is divided into two stages: the labor force participation stage and the employment stage. The first stage involves the decision to enter the labor force and begin actively seeking employment. The second involves the acquisition of employment. Each stage will be separately investigated. The effects and interactions between variables thought to be related to labor force participation and employment will be examined in a multivariate regression model that is adapted from a model developed by J. G. Anderson to explain health service utilization.[1]

Despite the problems that Indochinese refugees face in their search for employment, studies that have evaluated labor force participation rates (those who are not seeking employment versus those who are employed or seeking employment) and employment rates (those who are employed versus those who are seeking employment) among Indochinese refugees have generally been optimistic in their conclusions. Bach and Bach note in a study of pre-1978 arrivals that the refugee labor force participation rate is only slightly lower than the rate for the general population and the refugee employment rate is higher than the rate for the general population.[2] They also note that labor force participation and employment increase steadily with length of residence. R. E. March uses similar data and reaches similar conclusions.[3] Nevertheless, because the two groups are too different to allow it, both studies caution against optimistic expectations for recent arrivals based on early arrival data. Bach and Bach also indicate a need for more precise information on the effectiveness of resettlement programs and on ethnic differences in resettlement experiences.[4] More recent data from areas with higher refugee concentrations suggest that large proportions of "time-expired" refugees are remaining on public assistance.

The employment data that were obtained from the San Diego study are presented by length of residence and ethnicity in tables 8.1 and 8.2. The labor force participation rate in our sample is about 61 percent. The increase in participation associated with length of residence is dramatic but predictable, ranging from over 80 percent among early arrivals to less than 10 percent among recent arrivals. Only 6.5 percent of the 1976 and 1977 arrivals are not in the labor force. Ethnic differences in participation are less dramatic, ranging from 59 percent among the Lao to 67 percent among the Hmong.

The overall employment rate in our sample is 65 percent. Differences associated with length of residence are again dramatic but predictable: the employment rate among 1975 arrivals is over 90 percent and the rate among the 1980 arrivals is less than 35 percent. Ethnic differences in employment rates are more pronounced than they are in labor force participation rates. The Vietnamese have a 72 percent employment rate and the Cambodians have a 39 percent

Table 8.1 Labor force participation by length of residence and ethnicity

Labor force participation	Length of residence (in years		
	Less than 1 year	1	2
In labor force	8.0	46.5	64.7
Not in labor force	92.0	53.5	35.3
Total	75	213	235

employment rate. However, these differences may be overstated due to the relationship between ethnicity and length of residence. The Vietnamese have been here longer than refugees from the other three ethnic groups and can be expected to have a higher employment rate.

Labor Force Entry

Some preliminary indications as to why some refugees seek employment while others do not are provided by table 8.3. This table lists responses to an open-ended question that was asked of all refugee heads of household who were not seeking employment: "Why are you not currently looking for a job?" The most frequent response was English language deficiency. Overall, 42 percent of the nonparticipants cited their inability to speak English effectively, while 9 percent cited illness and 7.8 percent cited child care responsibilities. Response differences that are associated with length of residence are not dramatic, unlike those that are associated with ethnicity. Deficiencies in English language ability are substantially more pronounced for the Hmong and Cambodians. Illness is most pronounced among the Vietnamese and is not even present for the Lao. Child care is primarily a Vietnamese and Cambodian problem.

The twelve variables that were included in the multivariate regression analysis of the first stage in the employment process were

Table 8.2 Employment status by length of residence and ethnicity

Employment status	Length of residence (in years		
	Less than 1 year	1	2
Seeking employment	80.0	64.5	43.6
Employed	20.0	35.5	56.4
Total	5	93	149

			Ethnicity				
3	4–5	6	Vietnamese	Lao	Hmong	Cambodian	Total
68.7	93.5	87.9	60.0	58.5	67.0	59.4	60.5
30.3	6.5	12.1	40.0	41.5	33.0	40.6	39.5
89	46	132	430	159	100	101	790

placed into one of four categories: facilitating/program variables, enabling variables, predisposing variables, and ethnicity. The two facilitating/program variables focus on refugee awareness of job skills training programs and job placement programs. The six enabling variables focus on the ability of the refugee to actively seek employment. They are morbidity, subjective health, English language skill, length of residence, ESL enrollment, and automobile access. The three predisposing variables focus on demographic characteristics. These are age, home country education, and gender. Four dummy variables, one for each ethnic group, were created to measure the effect of ethnicity.

The order of entry of these variables in the equation is based on their degree of controllability and their proximity to the labor force entry decision. Thus, the facilitating/program variables are entered first, the enabling variables are entered second, the predisposing variables are entered third, and the ethnicity variables are entered last. The decision to enter the ethnicity variables last is based, in part, on the relationship between ethnicity and a number of the more proximate variables (e.g., home country education, length of residence, health status, etc.). If it were allowed to enter first it might mask the effects of these variables. The results of the regression analysis of labor force entry are given in table 8.4. This table contains the standardized and unstandardized regression coefficients, and standard

			Ethnicity				
3	4–5	6	Vietnamese	Lao	Hmong	Cambodian	Total
29.5	16.3	7.0	27.5	39.1	35.4	61.1	34.8
70.5	83.7	93.0	72.5	60.9	64.6	38.9	65.2
61	43	115	255	92	65	54	466

Table 8.3   Reasons for head of household not seeking employment by year of arrival by ethnicity (in percent)

	1975	1976–77	1978
None	5.9	20.0	3.4
Illness	35.3	0.0	24.1
Child care	11.8	20.0	27.6
Do not speak English	5.9	0.0	20.7
Other	41.2	20.0	17.2
Don't know/no answer	0.0	40.0	6.9

errors for the coefficients and equations. The equations are presented for (1) the entire sample, (2) recent arrivals (1979–81), (3) early arrivals (1975–78), and (4) each ethnic subsample. The R^2s in the equation range from .27 for early arrivals to .58 for the Lao.

In the overall equation, automobile availability (.23), English writing skills (.17), and ESL enrollment (−.17) are the best nonethnic predictors of labor force participation. The combination of a positive English writing coefficient and a negative ESL coefficient suggests that refugees who have better English language skills tend to enter the labor force while those who have worse English language skills tend to enroll in an ESL program in order to improve their skills. The automobile coefficient indicates that, while language skills are an important consideration in labor force entry, they are by no means the only one. Restricted access to transportation also prevents refugees from entry.

In this same equation, the negative coefficients associated with the Vietnamese and Lao variables indicate that there are ethnic differences in labor force participation that are independent of the influence of the other variables. Given their language ability and education, these two groups are less likely than the Hmong and Cambodians to be in the labor force. Hmong and Cambodian refugees with less developed job skills are apparently more willing to enter the labor force than their Vietnamese and Lao counterparts.

The impacts of English language skill and automobile availability are about the same for the early and recent arrival subgroups. The major differences between these groups appear to be in the areas of perceived health status and ESL enrollment. Among recent arrivals, ESL enrollment is competitive with labor force participation. This is not true among refugees who have been here for a longer period. Among this group, perceived health status emerges as the

1979	1980	1981	Vietnamese	Lao	Hmong	Cambodian	Overall
9.9	6.6	12.9	2.3	23.5	2.9	14.3	8.7
12.1	3.3	2.9	12.6	23.5	2.9	14.3	8.7
11.0	1.6	4.3	13.7	0.0	5.7	10.7	9.0
39.6	57.4	40.0	40.0	20.6	77.1	53.6	42.2
13.2	19.7	12.9	29.1	0.0	8.6	7.1	17.4
14.3	11.5	27.1	2.3	55.9	2.9	12.5	15.0

second most important predictor of labor force participation.

There are numerous ethnic differences in the predictors of labor force participation. The model is most effective in predicting participation for the Lao ($R^2 = .58$) and least effective in predicting it for the Cambodians ($R^2 = .36$). Furthermore, for the Cambodians, English language skills and automobile availability do not even enter the regression equation. For them, awareness of the availability of a job skills training program and length of residence are the most important predictors of participation. This fact reinforces the finding that there are ethnic differences in the labor force participation decision that are unrelated to ethnic differences in employability.

The limited effects of predisposing variables in the labor force participation equations is somewhat reassuring. It suggests that labor force entry can be described largely in terms of the more controllable variables. However, the uneven effects of the facilitating/program variables is not as reassuring. Awareness of job skills training or job placement services is an important factor in the decision to enter the labor force only for the Lao and Cambodians. The minimal effects of these variables in the Vietnamese and Hmong equations indicate that, among these groups, those who are looking for employment are no more likely than those who are not to be aware of the facilitating employment services.

Employment Status

The previous analysis provides a preliminary description of the conditions that prevent refugees from seeking employment. It does not provide a description of the conditions that lead to employment acquisition. Thus, a multivariate analysis based on the same model was also conducted to distinguish refugees who are employed from

Table 8.4 Results of labor force entry regression analysis on all Indochinese, early and recent arrivals, and on individual ethnic groups[a]

	All Indochinese			Recent arrivals (1979–81)		
	B	SEB	BETA	B	SEB	BETA
FACILITATING						
Awareness job skills training	.06	.03	.06	.11	.05	.11
Awareness job placement service	.13	.03	.13	.17	.05	.17
ENABLING						
ESL enrollment	−.16	.03	−.17	−.18	.05	−.16
Being treated by a doctor	−.13	.03	−.11	−.13	.05	−.11
English writing skills	.17	.03	.17	.14	.05	.14
Automobile availability	.22	.03	.23	.16	.04	.16
Perceived health status						
Length of residence						
PREDISPOSING						
Education in home country						
Gender	.12	.04	.09	.09	.05	.06
Age						
ETHNICITY						
Vietnamese	−.25	.03	−.26	−.34	.05	−.34
Lao	−.17	.04	−.14	−.23	.05	−.20
Hmong						
Cambodian						
R^2	.36	(SE = .155)		.32	(SE = .132)	

a. Estimates are given only when $p < .05$.

Early arrivals (1975–78)			Vietnamese			Lao			Hmong			Cambodian		
B	SEB	BETA	B	SEB	BETA	B	SEB	BETA	B	SEB	BETA	B	SEB	BETA
			.07	.04	.07	.18	.06	.18				.35	.09	.33
.08	.04	.11				.27	.06	.28	.08	.12	.06			
			−.12	.05	−.12	−.29	.06	−.28						
			−.15	.05	−.13	−.23	.09	−.15						
.11	.05	.13	.11	.05	.11	.15	.06	.16	.14	.12	.14			
.27	.06	.27	.20	.05	.20				.25	.09	.26			
.11	.03	.22							.10	.05	.17			
			.04	.01	.17	.09	.02	.23				.10	.03	.31
									.17	.08	.29			
.19	.06	.18	.13	.05	.10									
.27 (SE = .107)			.37 (SE = .155)			.58 (SE = .108)			.41 (SE = .142)			.36 (SE = .164)		

Table 8.5 Results of employment status regression analysis on all Indochinese, early and recent arrivals, and on individual ethnic groups[a]

	All Indochinese			Recent arrivals (1979–81)		
	B	SEB	BETA	B	SEB	BETA
FACILITATING						
Receive job skills training						
Use job placement service	−.25	.04	−.27			
ENABLING						
ESL enrollment	−.44	.05	−.46	−.53	.07	−.47
Being treated by a doctor						
English writing skills	.17	.05	.17	.20	.07	.19
Automobile availability	.25	.04	.26	.20	.07	.20
Perceived health status	.08	.02	.13	.09	.04	.14
Length of residence						
PREDISPOSING						
Education in home country	−.03	.01	−.10			
Gender						
Age						
ETHNICITY						
Vietnamese						
Lao						
Hmong						
Cambodian	.16	.06	.11			
R^2	.49	(SE = .118)		.42	(SE = .149)	

a. Estimates are given only when $p < .05$.

Early arrivals (1975–78)			Vietnamese			Lao			Hmong			Cambodian		
B	SEB	BETA	B	SEB	BETA	B	SEB	BETA	B	SEB	BETA	B	SEB	BETA
			−.30	.05	−.33									
−.22	.06	−.27	−.29	.06	−.33	−.64	.08	−.64	−.31	.12	−.26	−.94	.17	−.80
									−.54	.25	−.24			
									.53	.12	.54			
.25	.08	.27	.20	.06	.22	.20	.08	.20						
			.13	.03	.22	.13	.04	.22	−.22	.06	−.38			
			.04	.01	.21									
			−.03	.01	−.15									
−.01	.01	−.19												
.24 (SE = .10)			.43 (SE = .118)			.69 (SE = .076)			.50 (SE = .127)			.64 (SE = .090)		

those who are in the labor force, but without jobs. The only difference in variables is the substitution of job skills training and job placement awareness with job skills training and job placement use. We would expect the relative weights of the variables in each of the four categories to be different in these equations from what they were in the previous analysis.[5] The results of this analysis are given in table 8.5.

The R^2s in the seven equations range from .24 for early arrivals to .69 for the Lao. The only variable that is a significant predictor of employment in all seven equations is enrollment in an ESL course. In every case, those who are enrolled are less likely to be employed than those who are not enrolled. However, this does not necessarily indicate that lack of an English language communication skill is the only major barrier to refugee employment. The measured effect of this skill may be artificially exaggerated by the ESL variable as a result of local policy. Refugees who apply for public assistance in San Diego County are often required to enroll in an ESL program as a condition of receiving assistance. Thus the relationship between being unemployed and being enrolled in ESL may, at least in part, be an artifact of the relationship between being unemployed and being on public assistance. The relationship may also be exaggerated by job-seeking refugees who enroll in ESL while they are looking for a job because ESL courses are available to them and because they feel that better English language skills can be beneficial (though not necessary) for employment.

On the other hand, there is also evidence that the relationship is not spurious. First, the magnitude of the coefficients varies considerably from −.94 percent for the Cambodians to −.29 for the Vietnamese. Second, 22 percent of those who are employed are enrolled in ESL and 21 percent of those who are unemployed are not enrolled in ESL. Second, English writing skill is also related to employment in the general model. But because this relationship is significant in only one of the ethnic group models, it would appear that its presence in the general model is due primarily to the Hmong.

There is some evidence that the actual effect of English writing skills is understated in the other models due to the presence of the ESL variable. ESL and English writing skills are very closely related to each other and to employment status. Sixty-nine percent of those who have a limited writing skill are enrolled in an ESL course and only 29 percent of those who have a better skill are enrolled in an ESL course. Both are also closely related to employment status. The ESL/employment figures were given above. The English writing skill/ employment figures are as follows: 39 percent of those who have limited skills are employed and 78 percent of those who have better skills are employed. Thus, when ESL enters the equation the measured effect of English writing skills on employment will be reduced. It should also be noted that the measured effect of English writing skill is highest in the equation that has one of the lowest measured effects of ESL.

When considered jointly, the measured effects of these two variables indicate that English language skill is at minimum highly regarded by refugees as an employment asset. At a maximum, it would be extremely difficult to compensate for the lack of this skill. In either case, the emphasis on ESL seems justifiable.

The consistency of the measured effects of automobile ownership suggests that transportation is another major barrier to employment. However, the actual effect would be exaggerated by these measures if an automobile tended to be an initial purchase of employed refugees rather than a decisive purchase of job-seeking refugees. Technically, if this were the case, it could not be considered a barrier to employment. On the other hand, the fact that automobile ownership is consistently related to employment indicates, at a minimum, that refugees perceive transportation to be a sufficiently important problem to warrant resolution as soon as possible (i.e., as soon as employment is obtained). Indeed, over 90 percent of the employed refugees indicated that they drive an automobile to work and over 50 percent of the unemployed refugees who are not currently seeking employment cite transportation as a major reason for not seeking work.

Surprisingly, the use of job placement services was significant in only the overall model and among the Vietnamese, and the use of job skills training services was not significant in any of the seven equations. Again, this may be due to the relationship between the use of services and ESL enrollment. Fifty-five percent of those who had received job placement services were enrolled in ESL and 47 percent of those who had received job skills training were enrolled in ESL. It is likely that this interaction is suppressing the significance of these variables.

Perceived health status is a significant predictor of employment status in five of the equations. The early arrivals and the Cambodian equations are the only two where health status is not present. The coefficients range from .22 for the Hmong to −.08 for the overall equation.

Again, the lack of significant relationships between employment status and the predisposing variables provides encouraging evidence that employment status in the United States is determined by enabling variables and not by conditions that were determined prior to arrival. As further evidence of this, the less educated Vietnamese refugees experience slightly less difficulty in obtaining employment than the educated Vietnamese. This may be due to the lack of upgrading skills programs and underemployment among the educated groups.[6]

Conclusions

The results of this analysis indicate that a limited English language communication skill is a major barrier to labor force participation and employment, but not the only barrier. Transportation and health are barriers in both phases of the employment process.

The results also reveal two encouraging aspects of the language problem. First, those who have a limited skill are very likely to be enrolled in an ESL program and those who have a more developed skill are very likely to be in the labor force. The program is serving those who can benefit from it. Second, the effect of language decreases with length of residence. In the labor force participation model the effect of ESL enrollment is limited to recent arrivals and in the employment status model the effect of English language writing skill is limited to recent arrivals. Perhaps the combination of programs and contact are reducing the effect of the language problem.

Despite its encouraging implications for the language problem, the analysis does not indicate whether recent arrivals will experience greater or less difficulty than early arrivals in obtaining employment. It does indicate that employment barriers are different for early and recent arrivals, but does not reveal the source of the differences. It also indicates ethnic differences in employment experiences. Cambodians are the only group for which ESL enrollment is the only variable that distinguishes employed refugees from those who are seeking employment. The Vietnamese are the only group for which the unemployed have a higher awareness of the facilitating services than the employed. The Hmong are the only group for which English language writing skills are a major predictor of employment status, and for which home country education is a major predictor of labor force entry. And automobile availability is not a significant predictor of labor force entry for the Lao and Cambodians. These ethnic differences reveal a uniqueness in the employment-related experiences of the different groups that exists within the general context of a language problem. The magnitude of the differences indicates a possible need for employment programs that are tailored to the particular needs of specific ethnic groups.

9
The
Assimilation
Process

The goal of any policy of resettlement is the successful assimilation of refugees into the country of final asylum. This implies the integration of refugees into the cultural fabric of the host society. It also implies the resocialization of refugees into the political and social norms of the society. However, it does not in any sense imply the accommodation of refugees as suggested by Zangwill's "melting pot."[1] Indeed, the characteristics of the melting pot society have seldom been the American immigrant experience. In a pluralistic society such as this, assimilation is not characterized by a uniform culture. Therefore it is not likely that the cultural patterns of refugees will disappear. If the assimilation is successful, common goals and interests will develop over time.

There is much debate about the attributes and consequences of a resettlement policy directed toward assimilation. If assimilation is a process that is characterized by decreasing differentiation between subcultures and the dominant culture, then it may be impossible to distinguish between a socially well-adjusted refugee and a well-assimilated refugee.[2] More important, the present conceptualization of assimilation does not give any direction concerning the degree of conformity or commitment that is required for an "assimilated" classification of refugees. Should the Hmong be similar in outlook and motivation to other Americans? On the one hand, we find popular support for the abandonment of previous loyalties.[3] On the other hand, we find the broad criteria of the United Nations, which require merely loyalty and positive commitment to the host society.[4] Both conceptualizations are manifest in the policy discussions of Congress, but imply different sets of criteria for the design of programs to facilitate a resettlement effort having a goal of assimilation.

Although government policy certainly has an effect on the process of assimilation, an objective criterion for measuring assimilation has not been developed. In its absence, subjective measures of assimilation assume major significance in determining whether a resettlement policy is successful. Subjective measures such as problems of perception, the development of reciprocal relationships, identification, and affective feelings must be measured in the majority population as well as the immigrant group in order to assess the actual effectiveness of a resettlement program. Thus the problems of involuntary migrants are compounded by the nature of their immigration and the expectations of the host populations. The greater the dissimilarities between the refugees' culture and their hosts' culture, the less the likelihood of subjective acceptance of their assimilation.[5]

The status of the involuntary immigrant and the divergent expectations of the host population create a differential in resettlement outcomes. As indicated in previous chapters, some refugees experience acceptance while others experience discrimination and hardship. Some may become part of an "unassimilable" minority which is not considered part of the host society. This chapter provides some insights into the burdens that resettlement imposes on refugees and the barriers they perceive to be present in the assimilation process.

Resettlement and the Assimilation Process

The general studies of international migration have suggested a number of models that might be useful in understanding the problems that Indochinese refugees face in the assimilation process. In all models, the nature of the refugee experience is critical in understanding the problems of resettlement and assimilation. E. F. Kunz suggests that refugees who flee because of social upheaval may have a more difficult time in resettlement, whereas refugees who are anticipating changes are more likely to assimilate quickly.[6] Hansen and Oliver Smith suggest that political refugees will have the more difficult resettlement experience due to the unanticipated flight and the more positive images of their homeland.[7] Forced migration is an important distinguishing factor in the absence of a desire or motivation to leave a place of residence.[8] Consequently, migration becomes a means of escaping a life-threatening situation and is oriented toward the retention or re-establishment of past conditions.

Several models have been suggested as tools to explain the refugee resettlement and assimilation process. These models are not rigorous, but they do present explanations of how Western governments have approached the issue of resettlement. Although the models are presented as discrete explanations, there are invariably some overlaps in the actual implementation of government programs.

The traditional process of assimilation of immigrant populations best fits an enculturation model.[9] This model describes the process by which immigrants to American society experience a process of deculturation and "Americanization."[10] For voluntary immigrants, it is possible to anticipate the behavior and roles that allow them to fuse with the patterns of American culture. By denouncing the old culture, tradition, and behaviors, these immigrants may even over-identify with the symbols and norms of the host society. Over time, the result of their socialization process is the development of the reciprocal identification. Finally, intermarriage and social mobility accomplish the goal of assimilation.

It is important to note that the enculturation model provides no role for government authority. German, Irish, Italian, and other older ethnic groups experienced this process without federal support. The aid and assistance necessary for successful resettlement was provided by ethnic associations and voluntary agencies. In large cities, these ethnic associations provided the solidarity and social support needed to face the hostilities experienced in the larger society.[11] However, for involuntary migrants, this period of enculturation may be much longer, as they usually retain close ties with relatives in their native country and intend to return home at some point.[12]

In contrast to the enculturation model, a second partial explanation of the assimilation process emphasizes economic adaptation. Whereas the enculturation process focuses on cultural adaptation, the economic adaptation model stresses government intervention to promote the development of the resources and skills necessary for employment. In this model, language and interpersonal skills take precedence over enculturation problems.[13] The organization and structure of the resettlement effort are geared toward the goal of economic independence. Thus resettlement programs tend to orient the refugees toward previous work situations, most of which tend to be basic and manual.

The degree of assimilation is measured by the acquisition of the economic attributes of the dominant culture. In this model, language is not envisioned as a "carrier of culture" but a reliable index of employability.[14] Consequently, employment is viewed as a reliable index of assimilation because of the reciprocal identification that can be created in the workplace. Over time, the adjustment to the socioeconomic environment is enhanced by self-sufficiency.

A partial explanation that best represents the experiences of Asian-Americans is the ethnic enclave model. The history of Chinese and Japanese immigration shows heavy reliance on ethnic group solidarity.[15] By providing emotional and social support, these centers of ethnic concentration provide a bridge between the old culture and the demands of the new. Further, these ethnic enclaves allow the immigrants to turn inward in order to avoid a sometimes hostile host society.

The ethnic enclave is also important for the development of economic self-sufficiency. Ethnic group solidarity is translated into economic power as submarkets develop within the enclaves. Substantial economic and social progress toward assimilation is made only after economic development has occurred in the enclave. Subsequently, the upward mobility of third generation families accomplishes the assimilation into the host culture.[16]

Unlike the enculturation model, the ties to the old culture are much stronger. As in the case of the Japanese, the initial orientation is to return home once one has developed financial security.[17] However, in the case of the involuntary migrant this is not always possible. Given this condition, the degree of assimilation can be measured by the development of positive feeling toward the host society and the aggregate level of social class mobility.

Present U. S. resettlement policy can best be assessed as a hybrid of all three models. The present sponsorship system provides a degree of contact and economic security unknown to other immigrants. The goal of sponsorship is to accelerate the pace of the assimilation process. However, there has been a clear pattern of ethnic enclave development. These refugees are currently creating large enclaves which are similar in development to those of the Chinese and Japanese.

The critical assumption of all approaches is that economic and cultural contact and interaction will promote assimilation. Unfortunately, several factors might present barriers to successful economic adjustment. Language skills, employment skills, and racial prejudice are some of these factors. These barriers are especially notable in the case of forced migration where the host population has little preparation for the effects of the refugees' presence. In the case of the Indochinese population, feelings about the war and the downturn in the economy are certainly factors that create barriers to their assimilation. In addition, the diversity of previous experiences requires an examination of the nature of these barriers as perceived by each refugee group.

Refugee Perception of Assimilation

Recent changes in U. S. resettlement policy have focused the attention of social service delivery agencies on the issues of English language skill and employment. Unfortunately, these problem areas are not necessarily those of most concern to the refugees themselves. In addition, the four major refugee ethnic groups have different cultural traditions, education, and educational backgrounds, and were affected to differing degrees by the war. In order to gain a better understanding of what the refugees themselves perceive to be their most serious problems in resettlement, the respondents in the San Diego study were asked to rate the seriousness of each of twenty potential resettlement problem areas for themselves and their community. For each problem area, the respondent was asked whether it was considered very serious, somewhat serious, or not very serious. Table 9.1 gives the overall means and ranking of the twenty problem areas.

Not unexpectedly, the lack of English language skills ranked as the most serious problem overall. This finding is consistent with those of other studies, and with resettlement policies that emphasize the acquisition of English language skills as a necessary adjunct to employment and the achievement of economic self-sufficiency.[18] English language ability is also necessary for social interaction with Americans, which is essential for learning new culturally appropriate behaviors in the new society.

Family separation is ranked second overall. This finding is indicative of the great importance placed upon the extended family by the

Indochinese and is consistent with the results of an Illinois study in which family separation was the problem most frequently cited by refugees. Again, this is expected given the importance of family reunification in refugee secondary migration.[19] The effects of nearly thirty years of war and the often ardous and painful flight from one's home country are serious problems for many refugees, as seen in its ranking as the third most serious problem.

The next three problem areas are related to more general issues of employment and economic self-sufficiency. These three tend to cluster together in the top six problem areas across all four ethnic groups. The ranking of difficulties with American agencies and in understanding American life in the top ten problem areas is also consistent with Haines's overview of other Indochinese refugee survey data. These refugees come from a very different cultural context than that of the United States. Many lack experience with or knowledge of American culture. The lack of English language skills is a barrier to communication and cross-cultural understanding. A very high percentage of refugees apply for public assistance shortly after arrival. The complicated bureaucracy of the social service delivery system can be bewildering and somewhat intimidating for these refugees.

The lack of transportation and child care services is also considered important. Indeed, the lack of transportation is cited by more than 50 percent of the refugees who are not currently in the labor force as the major barrier to being there. Public transit can be confusing for refugees who are not familiar with the layout of the city or who lack the language ability to ask for assistance. Some of the Hmong respondents indicated that the distance of some social services from the Hmong community prevented many Hmong from utilizing them.

Some interesting differences emerge in an examination of individual ethnic group mean scores and rankings of problem areas. Money is ranked the number one problem by the Vietnamese. The cultural background of many Vietnamese, with its strong Confucianist influence, sanctions and encourages hard work, success, and responsibility for family members and, by extension, for the community.[20] Many of the first wave of Vietnamese refugees were middle-class managerial and professional people, and the downward occupational movement they have experienced in the

Table 9.1 Overall means and ranking of twenty problem areas

Not enough money
Difficulty in understanding American life
English language problem
War memories and departure from home
Separation from family members
Difficulty in getting good food
Lack of job skills training
Difficulty in practicing religion
Lack of ethnic support groups
Problems in raising children in U.S.
Alcohol or drug problems
Difficulty in getting information on daily living
American prejudice
Poor housing conditions
Lack of help in getting a job
Lack of child care services
Transportation problems
Difficulty with American agencies
Conflict between various refugee groups
Difficulty in correspondence with home country

United States has been a difficult transition.

The importance of the extended family and lineage is seen in the ranking of separation of family members as the second most serious problem for the Vietnamese refugees. The flight from Vietnam frequently entailed the separation of family members, and the U.S. resettlement policy favored nuclear families, contributing to the breakup of the traditional extended family. The war and the departure from Vietnam remain serious problems for many of the refugees.

Camp Pendleton, about forty-five miles north of San Diego, was the original reception center for many of the first wave of Vietnamese refugees who settled in San Diego. These refugees had higher rates of English language ability, more years of education, and greater exposure to American culture than subsequent waves. This may account for the relatively low ranking of problems with English (fourth) and of difficulties with American life (ninth).

One fact that clearly emerges from these data is that the Hmong

Overall		Vietnamese		Lao		Hmong		Cambodian	
Mean	Rank	Mean	Rank	Mean	Rank	Mean	Rank	Mean	Rank
1.555	4	1.377	1	1.579	4	1.020	1	2.700	10
1.975	8	2.123	9	1.866	7	1.091	4	2.355	7
1.371	1	1.512	4	1.214	1	1.060	3	1.336	3
1.539	3	1.509	3	1.974	11	1.515	13	1.064	1
1.420	2	1.432	2	1.706	5	1.270	8	1.091	2
2.734	19	2.972	19	2.665	18	1.667	16	2.864	15
1.688	6	1.908	6	1.345	2	1.040	2	1.891	5
2.791	20	2.988	20	2.625	17	2.253	18	2.782	12
2.061	11	2.130	10	1.955	9	1.102	5	2.817	14
2.223	13	2.192	12	2.232	15	1.473	12	2.945	17
2.653	18	2.443	16	2.897	20	2.592	19	2.972	19
2.289	15	2.401	15	2.236	16	1.650	15	2.518	8
2.194	12	2.355	14	2.007	12	1.173	6	2.794	13
2.236	14	2.344	13	2.063	14	1.465	10	2.764	11
1.561	5	1.569	5	1.520	3	1.060	3	2.037	6
2.051	10	2.015	7	1.973	10	1.394	9	2.879	16
2.015	9	2.080	8	1.809	6	1.470	11	2.560	9
1.923	7	2.162	11	1.879	8	1.182	7	1.752	4
2.597	17	2.728	18	2.693	19	1.598	19	2.972	19
2.411	16	2.550	17	2.038	13	1.786	17	2.963	18

perceive themselves as facing much greater problems in acculturation than the other refugee ethnic groups. Their means are much lower than the means for the other groups. Eighty percent of the problem areas are considered either somewhat serious or very serious by the Hmong. This is understandable, as the Hmong have the lowest literacy rates and the fewest years of education of all the refugee groups. Over 60 percent list their previous occupation as soldier. Their reliance upon a swidden agricultural economy has provided them with little or no readily transferable employment skills.

The Hmong place a high value on independence and self-sufficiency.[21] Their cultivation and trading of opium enabled them to become wealthier than the surrounding tribes.[22] In the United States, however, the Hmong have one of the highest rates of dependency and face the greatest problems in employment and English language acquisition. The Lao Family Community, the nationwide Hmong mutual assistance association, has strongly emphasized the importance of job skills training, as well as participation in ESL classes. These issues are reflected in the ranking of problem areas by the Hmong respondents. Money and the lack of job skills training were ranked first and second, respectively. The lack of help in finding employment and the lack of English language skills tied for third.

The next four problems are indicative of the sense of cultural isolation faced by the Hmong. The Hmong had the highest ranking of difficulties with American life, American prejudice, and difficulties with American agencies. The relatively low ranking of separation of family members could be a result of the highly fluid nature of Hmong household composition, which often fragmented through migratory movement.[23]

The incredible human devastation that accompanied the Pol Pot regime's reign of terror in Cambodia is still a major problem for Cambodian refugees. Memories of the war and the departure from home, and the separation of family members are the two top-ranked problems for these refugees. Many of the other problem areas are considered either not very serious or somewhat serious. These perceptions can possibly be explained in terms of the strong influence of Buddhism in Cambodian culture. The moral and ethical teachings of Buddhism stress consensus, compromise, and an exterior calm and acceptance of events.[24]

For the Lao, English and separation from family members are the two highest-ranking problem areas. Money and assistance in getting a job are also important. However, war memories and departure from home are not as serious for the Lao. This may reflect the heterogeneous nature of the culture in Laos, as the Hmong also ranked this problem area relatively low in comparison to the Vietnamese and Cambodians.

The overall ranking of problem areas by refugees is fairly consistent with the priorities of federal resettlement policy and state resettlement agencies. However, an examination of the individual ethnic group rankings does indicate differences between these groups. Consideration of these differences is important in explaining the varying degrees of success of these groups in their assimilation into American society.

Refugee Perceptions of Assimilation and Resettlement Policy

Although aspects of all the resettlement models are represented in

U. S. resettlement policy, the economic adaptation model provides a central focus for the policy. The major resettlement efforts are in the areas related to self-sufficiency. The areas include job training, job placement, and the acquisition of English language communication skills. Given this focus, it would appear that the policy is effective. As noted in a previous chapter, employment increases with length of residence, and English language skills are a major employment barrier.

However, if the model is descriptive of the resettlement process, the increased employment should correspond to a decrease in adjustment problems. Employment should increase over time and adjustment problems should decrease. Table 9.2 investigates the latter. It examines responses on three of the twenty problem areas that deal specifically with adjustment to life in the United States. These include adjustment to the American way of life, perceptions of American prejudice, and degree of difficulty in dealing with American agencies. The responses are given for each year of arrival.

The results in table 9.2 fail to show any consistent decrease in the perceived difficulty of dealing with these problem areas. Although 1975 arrivals are generally better integrated than the other groups (fewer among them perceive the problems in these areas to be very serious), there is no pattern of decrease from 1981 arrivals to 1976 arrivals, as the model would suggest. We must conclude, given these results, that a policy focus on self-sufficiency does not necessarily resolve other resettlement problems related to integration and assimilation.

Table 9.2   Assimilation by year of arrival

	Overall	1975	1976	1977	1978	1979	1980	1981
American way of life								
Very serious problem	34.1	17.4	50.0	41.7	51.2	40.0	35.3	12.0
Not very serious problem	32.9	50.8	25.0	25.0	27.8	27.9	28.4	28.0
American prejudice								
Very serious problem	24.6	22.7	55.6	41.7	33.3	21.3	24.2	12.0
Not very serious problem	42.6	51.5	22.2	25.0	37.8	36.7	45.6	56.0
American agencies								
Very serious problem	37.6	8.3	50.0	33.3	45.6	38.3	51.2	33.3
Not very serious problem	24.6	62.9	27.8	41.7	28.9	23.8	18.1	28.0

Conclusions

The shock of relocation is often manifest in an unwillingness to adjust to a new lifestyle. However, adaptation and accommodation are part of the heritage of Indochina. Historically, there has always been a sense of accommodation and eventual assimilation into a dominant culture. Despite these historical adaptations, these refugees have experienced many difficulties in adjusting to American life.

The empirical evidence presented in this chapter confirms the general conclusion that these refugees are unique in the American ethnic heritage. Their language problems and cultural heritage prevent their socialization into the norms of the society. Various resettlement agents can perpetuate the passing of values to the refugees. These agents of socialization include government programs and programs sponsored by other resettlement agencies. However, the fragmentation of our socialization effort has resulted in a less than positive view of American society.

Indochinese refugees seem to be following a process of assimilation that is characteristic of Asian populations. Like the Japanese and Chinese, the Indochinese are developing ethnic enclaves. These enclaves provide the social support necessary for adjusting to American life. The only drawback is that their process of assimilation may be slowed by a clustering that prevents their active participation in the political and economic fabric of this society.

10
Policy Assessments and Recommendations

The refugee settlement program has grown in complexity and sophistication as states, counties, voluntary agencies, service providers, and refugees cope with conflicting federal program directives, shifting international priorities, and continuing fiscal uncertainties. All this is occurring in an economic climate that forces the local poor and the refugees to compete against each other in the low-paying job market as well as for the scarce cash, medical assistance, and social services that are available.

Indochinese refugee resettlement is complicated by many factors that reflect the differing interests and interrelationships that exist between the federal agencies, state administrations, county governments, voluntary agencies, service providers, and the multicultural refugees. In assessing the policy, the various components of resettlement are seen to provide a useful tool for the evaluation of present policy. In this chapter, an assessment is made of immigration policy, federal policy, state policy, and recent policy changes. In addition, policy recommendations are suggested with might improve the resettlement experiences of these involuntary migrants.

Assessment of Refugee Immigration Policy

Passage of the 1980 Refugee Act incorporates into law a definition relating to the status of a refugee. It defines a refugee as a person who has been persecuted or has a well-founded fear of persecution on account of race, religion, nationality, membership in a particular social group, or political opinion. The act also mandates regular consultations and yearly refugee admission ceilings. Fifty thousand is considered the annual "normal flow" of refugees into the United States, with larger numbers requiring prior consultation and agreement between the executive and legislative branches of government. A new priority system for admission replaces the category system that had been in effect since 1977. The new priorities stress, for Indochinese refugees, resettlement of those closely associated with former regimes in their home countries or the U.S. government, and those with relatives in the United States.

Prior to September 1981, applicants for resettlement from Indochina had been presumed to meet the definition of a refugee. In September 1981 the attorney general announced a return to case-by-case adjudication of Indochinese refugee applicants by the INS, claiming it was no longer appropriate to confer "categorical eligibility" to all Indochinese who have fled their homelands. The effect of the case-by-case approach has been a decline in actual admissions as compared to allowable admissions. In FY80, the ceiling for all refugees was 231,000, with 212,000 actual arrivals; the FY81 ceiling was 217,000, with 159,000 arriving; and the FY82 ceiling was 173,000, with 97,000 arriving. The FY83 ceiling was 90,000, with a projected actual arrival figure of between 60,000 and 63,000.[1] Approval rates for resettlement have ranged from 61 percent for the Cambodians to 87 percent for the Vietnamese.

A growing number of Indochinese refugees in first asylum camps began to be perceived as "economic migrants" or "intending immigrants." These terms were used increasingly to describe Cambodians who had been arriving in increasing numbers and congregating along the Thai border as well as within the Thai camps. Disputes have occurred between the State Department, the Justice Department, and the INS in interpreting refugee status policy. While the State Department condemns the Vietnamese for internal repression and invasion of Cambodia, INS officials have determined that resettlement applicants from the border areas are not refugees and could safely return to their homes without fear of persecution.

In late 1982 the attorney general also approved a reorganization of INS, elevating the position associated with refugees and creating the Office of the Executive Associate Commissioner to supervise overseas offices. In an attempt to emphasize interagency relationships, regular meetings have been scheduled between the Department of State and the INS to identify and seek resolutions to problems as they develop.

Criticism of the present refugee definition as contained in the act is made by those wishing to expand the definition to include persons fleeing civil war, famine, or other such life-threatening situations, in order to grant these people safe haven. The other side of the redefinition question is held by those wanting to tighten the definition to effectively exclude people who are motivated by economic considerations in leaving their homelands.

The Coordinator of Refugee Affairs, Ambassador H. Eugene Douglas, the third such administrator to hold the office since its creation in 1979, stated that the definition currently included in the 1980 act represents a political and substantive compromise that could be used to accommodate diverse interest groups and viewpoints. However, the present administration feels that reopening the debate on refugee definition could stall refugee resettlement efforts and stymie progress toward trying to internationalize the refugee population.[2]

While the United Nations High Commissioner on Refugees (UNHCR) has attempted to focus attention on the residual refugee population in camps in Southeast Asia, UNHCR officials have expressed the belief that local solutions, resettlement in first asylum countries, or returning to their homelands is almost impossible for Southeast Asians. Thus the High Commissioner has urged the United States to keep its immigration resettlement ceilings high for Indochinese.[3]

Assessment of Federal Policies

Federal policy is responsible for the admission of refugees and their resettlement. The close association between the U.S. government and the defeated South Vietnamese government, as well as humanitarian and international political considerations shaped initial federal actions in support of Indochinese evacuation and resettlement. Prior to the establishment of the Refugee Act of 1980, the resettlement of these refugees was carried out under ad hoc parole programs. Federal policy emphasized heavy involvement of voluntary agencies and the private sector. Although this emphasis minimized the expansion of the federal bureaucracy, it did not anticipate the large number of refugees who would continue to seek resettlement in the United States after 1975. Frequent extensions of the parole programs between 1975 and 1979 could not accommodate effective program monitoring.[4]

Resettlement efforts tended to be piecemeal responses to specific and recurring crises in refugee camps in countries of first asylum. Indochinese refugees who came to the United States did not need proof of persecution. The definition of a refugee included anyone who left a Communist country.

Reinforced by high refugee dependency rates, federal policy makers began to review resettlement policy. They concluded that there were no incentives for refugees to become self-sufficient. States did not have incentives to provide self-sufficiency directed programs as long as federal funding for cash and medical assistance was not limited. These conclusions resulted in a time limitation for federal government reimbursement of resettlement costs. The limitation was intended to reduce federal resettlement costs by reducing refugee dependence. Prior to this decision, the only required contributions of states and local governments to this federal effort were the costs of implementing service delivery systems and the management of tensions that the presence of these refugees brought to their economic and social environments. They were, after the decision, being asked to pay for the resettlement costs of "time-expired" refugees as well.

Some of the data indicating an increasing dependency rate among Indochinese refugees was in fact created by the federal policy of removing early arrival refugees from the data used to calculate the dependency rate.[5] The dependency rates that have been calculated after April 1981, when the thirty-six-month limit for cash and medical assistance became effective, have been based on the population of refugees who have lived in the United States less than three years. Previous dependency rate calculations included the entire Southeast Asian refugee population. And earlier arrivals were in fact participating in the labor force with greater frequency than the general U.S. population.

The 1980 act also mandated that cash assistance be contingent upon willingness to register for and accept employment after sixty days in the United States. In recognition of the lower wages paid to refugees, a portion of their wages was exempted from the calculation of eligibility. Finally, in order to address continuing criticisms from the Government Accounting Office concerning lack of accountability and coordination of services, the act required states to submit resettlement plans describing the nature and scope of their programs in order to receive federal resettlement funds.

Assessment of State Policies

A study prepared for ORR by Berkeley Planning Associates investigated the resettlement roles and perceptions of states. States were found to be active in the definition of program priorities and in the design and selection of service delivery mechanisms. They also complained that they did not have control of the refugee resettlement program. States cited lack of initial involvement in refugee placement, shifts in federal funding without adequate state input, delays in appropriated funding, and changing federal regulations for determining eligibility for cash and medical assistance as problems leading to their inability to manage and control refugee resettlement.[6]

Given this environment, states have attempted to maintain flexibility in their structuring of refugee assistance so they can react to shifting federal decisions. While the study found that states generally had adequate administrative competence, many decisions concerning the direction of refugee programming were left up to service providers contracted by the states on a continuing ad hoc basis.

States did not have enough summary data on program achievements to propose directions that would foster self-sufficiency and the reduction of cash and medical assistance programs. Their inability to evaluate program effectiveness has also been due to a lack of performance standards that, until recently, have not been provided by the federal government.[7]

The California State Coordinator for Refugee programs testified at the resettlement reauthorization hearing in 1982 that the refugee resettlement program was hampered by federal administration of the program as though it were temporary. This contributed to program uncertainties, unpredictability, and the lack of coherent policy. He felt that the program could be improved by a clear, credible, long-term commitment on the part of the federal government to accept full financial responsibility for providing the economic assistance and social services that are needed by refugees to achieve self-sufficiency.

A variety of recent policy change proposals by ORR have also increased the anxiety of states and localities that the federal government was backing away from full federal responsibility for resettlement. In 1981, ORR proposed an eighteen-month limit on assistance to refugees who do not qualify under a state's AFDC or General Assistance programs. This was intended to discourage refugees from viewing resettlement as a long-term program and, in part, to meet ORR's budget requirements. In October 1982 amendments were added to the law that were designed to provide closer oversight and increase consultations among those involved in the resettlement process. Under the amendments, voluntary agencies must notify welfare departments when refugees are offered employment. Refugee assistance is terminated if the refugee refuses employment. In addition, voluntary agencies must be notified by welfare agencies when a refugee receives assistance so the voluntary agency can renew efforts to help the refugee become self-sufficient. The amendments also eliminated the sixty-day grace period for employment registration and made registration with an appropriate employment service a condition for receiving cash assistance. Refugees also lost their one-third income disregard, and full-time college students were no longer eligible for cash assistance. These changes were an attempt to establish equity between the assistance available to refugees and nonrefugees and to increase employment incentives for refugees. In fact, they shifted many of the resettlement burdens to states that were already anxious about the federal government's commitment.

In sum, a great variety of organizational structures and practices have developed as each state attempts to make the resettlement plan consistent with its own welfare system and to respond to federal policy changes. Major differences regarding the coordination of responsibilities between the state and local service providers, the mechanisms that are used for service delivery and monitoring, and collection and analysis of service outcome data have evolved. Other differences accounting for variance among state programs are local economic conditions, the existence of other minorities in refugee communities, and the geographic distribution of refugees within the states.[8]

Policy Recommendations

Given the frequent criticisms and policy changes that have occurred in our nine-year experience with Indochinese refugee resettlement, it is apparent that our resettlement policy leaves much to be desired. The following discussion offers a series of recommendations that may be useful in shaping our future policy as well as future research. The recommendations are not exhaustive, but concentrate on the general objectives of current resettlement policy.

The first area of concern is the definition and admission of refugees. Discrimination between refugees and other migrants is the first critical step in a chain of events that leads to immigration and resettlement. The following recommendations seem appropriate:

1.   Definitions should be explicit as to the criteria that define the political refugee. In cases of rejection, there should be an appeal process coordinated by the countries that are resettling Indochinese refugees. The application of an explicit definition should respond to criticisms that those who are entering the United States are actually "economic migrants" or "intended immigrants." It should also eliminate Indochinese perceptions that other criteria are acceptable for admission.

2.   The power to confer refugee status should be shared between the former refugees and the INS. The inclusion of the refugee will lend legitimacy and consistency to the selection of potential immigrants.

3.   The activities of the voluntary agencies and the INS should be coordinated in the refugee camps. The selection, placement, and training of refugees should be a shared responsibility of public and private authorities.

4.   In the case of Indochinese refugees, the United States should seek support for local resettlement in Indochina and provide the appropriate funds for that effort if suitable locations are found.

5.   Support and assistance should be given to the UNHCR's efforts toward voluntary repatriation, provided safe conduct can be guaranteed and maintained.

6.   Orderly departure programs are needed to minimize the risks of migration. Diplomatic efforts should be directed at gaining Vietnam's acceptance and respect for orderly migration from the countries of Vietnam, Laos, and Cambodia.

The second set of recommendations is directed at federal responsibilities in program design. The scope and nature of federal authority is the central concern:

7. The federal government should assume complete responsibility for the resettlement of refugees. This includes financial as well as placement responsibility. To do otherwise has the effect of "politicizing" resettlement and creating animosities in situations that are already stressful.

8. The federal government should provide "up front" funding of self-sufficiency programs before refugees are allowed to participate in state welfare programs.

9. State governments that are adversely affected by secondary migration should be reimbursed by the federal government when state general assistance funds are used for refugees.

10. Federal authorities should monitor and evaluate state programs and their performance. Every effort should be made to reduce inconsistencies in implementing resettlement policy and to distinguish resettlement policy from welfare policies of the states. Inconsistent implementation is a major factor in secondary migration.

11. Coordination of the activities of the voluntary agencies in placement and resettlement is necessary for accelerating the movement toward self-sufficiency. Experimental resettlement programs should be encouraged. The results may be helpful to general resettlement policy.

A third area of concern is the response of state and local officials to national resettlement policy. The variations in state expenditure and policy orientation have been manifest in various resettlement programs. To remedy this situation, the following policy changes are suggested:

12. State policies should be coordinated by strong federal leadership in order to reduce the variation in the delivery of social services.

13. The developing refugee community associations should be included in the organization of any local resettlement effort.

14. State policies should include a component emphasizing the mobilization of financial resources within the refugee

community for economic self-sufficiency.

15.   State and local communities should be given adequate impact aid to withstand the impact of a large refugee population on the local social service delivery system.

16.   Resettlement programs should be responsive to the ethnic differences among refugees. Program effectiveness could be enhanced by focusing on these differences.

17.   The language barrier deserves more consistent emphasis in ESL programs. Cultural differences in the language acquisition process must be recognized in order to deal effectively with English language illiteracy among the less educated refugees.

18.   Health promotion efforts to improve health behaviors would ease the burden of medical care support for refugees.

19.   Resettlement programs should be directed toward community economic development. Self-reliance in a community setting may ensure self-confidence and social support.

In sum, these recommendations are only part of the general changes necessary to develop a more effective resettlement policy. Of course, such changes require political action for adoption. Unfortunately the temporary status of the resettlement program interferes with the momentum that would be needed for policy change.

Conclusions

The above recommendations are only a partial list of the policy changes that are being suggested by voluntary agencies, state agencies, and federal officials. Each recommendation addresses a key problem in the resettlement experience. What is required is a rethinking of present resettlement policy in light of the problems suggested elsewhere as well as in previous chapters of this book.

We have noted the dissimilarities of these refugees from previous American experiences. They range from the rural illiterate to the brightest minds of a modern society. They are involuntary migrants from the destruction of several social systems. Without choice, they have arrived in a new society where their old values and practices are ineffective.

We have also presented a picture of a fragmented government policy. At both state and federal levels, we have found unsystematic and poorly implemented policies—policies that create problems due to their variation in impact. Consequently, several states have assumed a disporportionate responsibility for placement and absorption of these refugees. The results have been less than desirable given the intentions of federal policy.

Finally, we have noted that the problems of assimilation and self-sufficiency have not been reduced by federal policy or length of U.S. residence. Problems persist in the face of discontinuous and temporary policy responses. What we have discussed in this book can best be described as a failure in policy formulation. Rather than the formulation of a coherent response to this policy problem, the policy has created barriers for some refugees and opportunities for others. In essence, our understanding of the problems of these refugees must stem from these mistakes.

Appendix A

**Refugee Arrival by Year,
State of Primary Migration,
and Ethnicity**

STATE	CAMBODIA	LAOS	VIETNAM	OTHER	TOTAL
1975					
Alabama	61	0	1420	0	1481
Alaska	1	0	74	0	75
Arizona	50	0	1341	0	1391
Arkansas	98	0	2775	0	2873
California	1498	8	24550	0	26056
Colorado	105	4	1988	0	2097
Connecticut	60	0	1129	0	1189
Delaware	4	0	160	0	164
District of Columbia	58	0	839	0	897
Florida	91	0	5629	0	5720
Georgia	30	0	1464	0	1494
Guam	0	0	247	0	247
Hawaii	20	0	807	0	827
Idaho	9	0	306	0	315
Illinois	165	2	4090	0	4257
Indiana	41	0	1924	0	1965
Iowa	66	48	2427	0	2541
Kansas	27	5	1902	0	1934
Kentucky	22	0	985	0	1007
Louisiana	113	0	4268	0	4381
Maine	22	0	388	0	410
Maryland	248	0	2263	0	2511
Massachusetts	54	0	1195	0	1249
Michigan	67	0	2401	0	2468
Minnesota	109	0	4123	0	4232
Mississippi	4	0	481	0	485

STATE	CAMBODIA	LAOS	VIETNAM	OTHER	TOTAL
Missouri	68	0	3180	0	3248
Montana	2	0	214	0	216
Nebraska	40	0	1311	0	1351
Nevada	2	0	384	0	386
New Hampshire	1	0	166	0	167
New Jersey	32	0	1709	0	1741
New Mexico	15	0	1124	0	1139
New York	152	6	4298	0	4456
North Carolina	5	0	1394	0	1399
North Dakota	24	0	427	0	451
Ohio	48	0	3117	0	3165
Oregon	474	0	1681	0	2155
Pennsylvania	387	6	7995	0	8388
Puerto Rico	0	0	1	0	1
South Carolina	30	0	221	0	251
South Dakota	21	0	842	0	863
Tennessee	13	0	579	0	592
Texas	34	4	1148	0	1186
Utah	412	2	9789	0	10203
Vermont	124	1	576	0	701
Virgin Islands	30	0	4019	0	4049
Virginia	235	1	4157	0	4393
Washington	321	4	4116	0	4441
West Virginia	12	11	214	0	237
Wisconsin	58	1	1972	0	2031
Wyoming	4	0	140	0	144
Unknown	4	5	158	5	172
TOTAL	5571	108	124108	5	129792

1976

Alabama	4	57	11	1	73
Arizona	0	62	1	2	65
Arkansas	0	48	10	1	59
California	211	1005	344	63	1623
Colorado	6	117	15	3	141
Connecticut	0	35	5	1	41
Delaware	0	0	0	0	0
District of Columbia	1	3	3	0	7
Florida	0	65	12	3	80
Georgia	0	57	20	2	79
Guam	0	0	0	3	3
Hawaii	0	437	26	11	474

STATE	CAMBODIA	LAOS	VIETNAM	OTHER	TOTAL
Idaho	0	8	0	1	9
Illinois	13	110	20	2	145
Indiana	0	35	42	2	79
Iowa	1	55	8	0	64
Kansas	0	24	0	0	24
Kentucky	0	50	11	0	61
Louisiana	0	51	8	2	61
Maine	0	5	2	0	7
Maryland	22	19	11	0	52
Massachusetts	0	12	2	2	16
Michigan	0	41	17	2	60
Minnesota	0	49	11	2	62
Mississippi	0	13	0	0	13
Missouri	1	25	3	1	30
Montana	8	18	1	0	27
Nebraska	0	55	3	5	63
Nevada	0	11	5	2	18
New Hampshire	0	0	0	0	0
New Jersey	2	13	1	0	16
New Mexico	0	15	9	1	25
New York	0	43	37	7	87
North Carolina	0	24	3	0	27
North Dakota	0	6	1	0	7
Ohio	1	73	12	4	90
Oklahoma	0	38	8	1	47
Oregon	1	30	4	4	39
Pennsylvania	1	59	18	4	82
Rhode Island	3	8	0	0	11
South Carolina	0	0	5	1	6
South Dakota	2	13	0	1	16
Tennessee	0	30	1	1	32
Texas	26	115	65	11	217
Utah	0	28	21	1	50
Vermont	0	0	0	0	0
Virginia	15	9	30	0	54
Washington	21	75	7	1	104
West Virginia	0	0	0	0	0
Wisconsin	0	107	0	0	107
Wyoming	0	0	0	0	0
TOTAL	339	3153	813	148	4453

STATE	CAMBODIA	LAOS	VIETNAM	OTHER	TOTAL
1977					
Alabama	0	0	6	0	6
Alaska	0	0	7	0	7
Arizona	0	6	17	1	24
Arkansas	0	7	12	2	21
California	6	10	1041	31	1088
Colorado	0	11	58	2	71
Connecticut	0	0	37	0	37
Delaware	0	0	3	1	4
District of Columbia	7	5	28	4	44
Florida	0	4	106	5	115
Georgia	0	1	35	1	37
Hawaii	1	5	28	1	35
Idaho	0	0	7	0	7
Illinois	1	14	78	4	97
Indiana	0	3	45	1	49
Iowa	1	4	18	2	25
Kansas	0	14	30	1	45
Kentucky	0	8	11	0	19
Louisiana	0	4	271	7	282
Maine	0	0	5	1	6
Maryland	1	10	25	2	38
Massachusetts	0	5	6	0	11
Michigan	0	1	41	2	44
Minnesota	0	0	58	2	60
Mississippi	0	0	0	0	0
Missouri	0	6	40	0	46
Montana	0	6	5	0	11
Nebraska	0	4	26	2	32
Nevada	0	0	4	0	4
New Hampshire	0	0	3	0	3
New Jersey	0	0	10	1	11
New Mexico	0	0	60	5	65
New York	9	22	351	17	399
North Carolina	1	0	3	1	5
North Dakota	0	0	4	0	4
Ohio	0	11	16	1	28
Oklahoma	2	0	21	1	24
Oregon	0	1	63	0	64
Pennsylvania	3	7	52	4	66
Rhode Island	0	0	0	0	0
South Carolina	0	0	27	0	27
South Dakota	0	2	18	2	22

STATE	CAMBODIA	LAOS	VIETNAM	OTHER	TOTAL
Tennessee	0	2	18	0	20
Texas	0	16	388	9	413
Vermont	0	0	0	0	0
Virginia	4	1	33	3	41
Washington	6	7	132	9	154
West Virginia	0	0	0	0	0
Wisconsin	0	16	52	3	71
Wyoming	0	0	7	0	7
TOTAL	44	213	3333	128	3718

1978

	CAMBODIA	LAOS	VIETNAM	OTHER	TOTAL
Alabama	8	103	73	9	193
Alaska	0	0	14	0	14
Arizona	0	39	148	5	192
Arkansas	3	57	118	8	186
California	230	1740	4080	287	6337
Colorado	84	315	241	53	693
Connecticut	31	111	145	23	310
Delaware	0	2	0	0	2
District of Columbia	19	80	212	8	319
Florida	22	80	401	14	517
Georgia	11	55	95	8	169
Hawaii	1	295	220	25	541
Idaho	0	37	9	1	47
Illinois	49	400	595	67	1111
Indiana	18	66	122	11	217
Iowa	3	202	78	20	303
Kansas	33	92	176	18	319
Kentucky	2	62	98	5	167
Louisiana	4	34	496	14	548
Maine	0	0	23	0	23
Maryland	8	30	200	7	245
Massachusetts	2	49	147	14	212
Michigan	33	99	246	20	398
Minnesota	50	306	318	46	720
Mississippi	0	6	87	3	96
Missouri	13	57	208	11	289
Montana	13	88	26	7	134
Nebraska	9	65	96	8	178
Nevada	2	59	100	11	172
New Hampshire	0	0	0	0	0
New Jersey	0	4	86	5	95

STATE	CAMBODIA	LAOS	VIETNAM	OTHER	TOTAL
New Mexico	4	63	147	12	226
New York	33	313	726	48	1120
North Carolina	0	95	56	12	163
North Dakota	15	0	32	3	50
Ohio	2	157	131	32	322
Oklahoma	14	90	261	25	390
Oregon	46	283	417	38	784
Pennsylvania	19	350	624	62	1055
Rhode Island	38	206	26	41	311
South Carolina	1	40	9	7	57
South Dakota	12	23	29	4	68
Tennessee	13	245	182	23	463
Texas	124	786	1491	113	2514
Utah	24	141	142	17	324
Vermont	0	0	1	0	1
Virginia	21	88	355	13	477
Washington	85	261	431	61	838
West Virginia	0	5	5	1	11
Wisconsin	6	247	129	35	417
Wyoming	0	0	1	0	1
TOTAL	1105	7926	14053	1255	24339

1979

Alabama	79	170	409	55	713
Alaska	0	9	41	2	52
Arizona	54	197	574	47	872
Arkansas	6	212	437	31	686
California	2604	4725	21067	1847	30243
Colorado	186	762	875	146	1969
Connecticut	156	402	557	89	1204
Delaware	0	24	35	3	62
District of Columbia	143	235	1088	67	1533
Florida	226	250	1621	106	2203
Georgia	141	284	698	58	1181
Hawaii	9	639	1428	129	2205
Idaho	4	99	82	14	199
Illinois	416	1575	2191	295	4477
Indiana	140	231	624	61	1056
Iowa	137	895	695	143	1870
Kansas	73	335	640	63	1111
Kentucky	16	168	229	25	438
Louisiana	28	195	1148	56	1427

STATE	CAMBODIA	LAOS	VIETNAM	OTHER	TOTAL
Maine	2	10	195	9	216
Maryland	121	67	683	27	898
Massachusetts	104	215	984	84	1387
Michigan	325	438	1163	103	2029
Minnesota	257	1449	1724	320	3750
Mississippi	16	44	284	16	360
Missouri	52	129	872	53	1106
Montana	5	231	153	40	429
Nebraska	34	185	284	48	551
Nevada	3	100	372	29	504
New Hampshire	1	31	43	7	82
New Jersey	35	93	693	61	882
New Mexico	24	180	434	34	672
New York	172	742	2835	259	4008
North Carolina	69	241	782	61	1153
North Dakota	39	71	117	9	236
Ohio	108	375	980	99	1562
Oklahoma	113	360	978	100	1551
Oregon	331	1182	1322	294	3129
Pennsylvania	675	991	2469	292	4427
Rhode Island	171	371	75	66	683
South Carolina	40	64	252	16	372
South Dakota	77	58	153	15	303
Tennessee	288	710	539	97	1634
Texas	608	1787	4812	439	7646
Utah	129	531	899	115	1674
Vermont	0	8	12	2	22
Virginia	227	307	1592	80	2206
Washington	836	1158	2246	314	4554
West Virginia	9	34	80	9	132
Wisconsin	130	814	492	131	1567
Wyoming	0	31	59	6	96
Unknown	3	0	3	0	6
TOTAL	9422	24414	63020	6472	103328

1980

	CAMBODIA	LAOS	VIETNAM	OTHER	TOTAL
Alabama	43	380	324	66	813
Alaska	9	34	97	4	144
Arizona	61	371	681	83	1196
Arkansas	17	365	577	50	1009
California	4231	10132	29630	2879	46872
Colorado	236	974	1071	174	2455

STATE	CAMBODIA	LAOS	VIETNAM	OTHER	TOTAL
Connecticut	166	761	612	105	1644
Delaware	0	46	44	1	91
District of Columbia	276	929	1228	118	2551
Florida	254	595	1770	115	2734
Georgia	102	1107	1079	108	2396
Hawaii	38	616	1113	114	1881
Idaho	12	182	116	24	334
Illinois	589	3037	2600	420	6646
Indiana	97	521	729	86	1433
Iowa	96	1475	726	170	2467
Kansas	51	603	1001	81	1736
Kentucky	40	257	321	27	645
Louisiana	36	135	2027	74	2272
Maine	44	73	173	16	306
Maryland	188	192	944	73	1397
Massachusetts	208	1338	1921	218	3685
Michigan	330	906	1525	181	2942
Minnesota	358	3748	2107	478	6691
Mississippi	3	29	330	22	384
Missouri	89	398	997	88	1572
Montana	8	249	72	21	350
Nebraska	37	244	354	34	669
Nevada	14	113	410	33	570
New Hampshire	14	81	35	9	139
New Jersey	28	299	1229	82	1638
New Mexico	26	706	419	87	1238
New York	296	1346	3328	353	5323
North Carolina	92	543	922	89	1646
North Dakota	30	163	48	29	270
Ohio	168	949	1066	180	2363
Oklahoma	112	639	1097	149	1997
Oregon	413	2925	1902	432	5672
Pennsylvania	512	1579	3223	310	5624
Rhode Island	163	641	85	63	952
South Carolina	38	199	292	35	564
South Dakota	38	140	113	26	317
Tennessee	60	949	413	82	1504
Texas	805	2411	7550	579	11345
Utah	224	1553	1144	248	3169
Vermont	18	109	61	14	202
Virginia	303	613	2282	153	3351
Washington	946	2788	3186	535	7455
West Virginia	14	117	142	26	299
Wisconsin	63	1391	499	120	2073

STATE	CAMBODIA	LAOS	VIETNAM	OTHER	TOTAL
Wyoming	0	75	39	13	127
Puerto Rico	0	5	0	0	5
TOTAL	11996	50031	83654	9477	155158

1981

STATE	CAMBODIA	LAOS	VIETNAM	OTHER	TOTAL
Alabama	321	120	280	62	783
Alaska	4	11	21	1	37
Arizona	576	147	300	90	1113
Arkansas	62	167	329	25	583
California	7125	5173	21111	2007	35416
Colorado	324	275	763	88	1450
Connecticut	378	312	430	50	1170
Delaware	3	7	23	2	35
District of Columbia	580	662	933	94	2269
Florida	551	358	1323	126	2358
Georgia	924	465	1358	121	2868
Hawaii	64	555	577	64	1260
Idaho	31	254	81	21	387
Illinois	1861	1330	1531	305	5027
Indiana	171	162	257	42	632
Iowa	239	587	495	71	1392
Kansas	176	308	1104	54	1642
Kentucky	125	82	281	23	511
Louisiana	207	226	1620	95	2148
Maine	203	73	91	42	409
Maryland	264	65	452	55	836
Massachusetts	1521	568	1828	252	4169
Michigan	293	230	754	68	1345
Minnesota	884	1158	1132	208	3382
Mississippi	6	18	205	5	234
Missouri	456	650	799	111	2016
Montana	10	41	17	7	75
Nebraska	97	78	312	25	512
Nevada	139	27	157	25	348
New Hampshire	44	23	41	4	112
New Jersey	116	139	624	41	920
New Mexico	119	340	552	49	1060
New York	2161	654	2439	380	5634
North Carolina	184	189	399	47	819
North Dakota	87	70	99	16	272
Ohio	809	421	640	131	2001
Oklahoma	314	385	768	77	1544

STATE	CAMBODIA	LAOS	VIETNAM	OTHER	TOTAL
Oregon	861	1272	1250	210	3593
Pennsylvania	1437	735	2259	299	4730
Rhode Island	463	368	217	70	1118
South Carolina	146	221	243	40	650
South Dakota	36	24	39	10	109
Tennessee	371	471	184	54	1080
Texas	3918	1896	4906	628	11348
Utah	579	481	522	85	1667
Vermont	6	25	22	3	56
Virginia	1099	328	1304	171	2902
Washington	1492	1360	2211	358	5421
West Virginia	5	36	44	1	86
Wisconsin	82	410	331	52	875
Wyoming	21	9	12	5	47
TOTAL	31945	23966	57673	6870	120454

1982

STATE	CAMBODIA	LAOS	VIETNAM	OTHER	TOTAL
Alabama	122	8	194	37	361
Alaska	0	1	19	0	20
Arizona	168	27	191	36	422
Arkansas	42	17	196	12	267
California	2291	1549	11313	863	16016
Colorado	211	84	534	57	886
Connecticut	158	44	335	21	558
Delaware	2	6	10	1	19
District of Columbia	295	113	490	76	974
Florida	357	78	905	88	1428
Georgia	315	134	870	95	1414
Hawaii	30	87	407	52	576
Idaho	45	28	133	13	219
Illinois	568	397	1102	187	2254
Indiana	84	50	222	27	383
Iowa	87	122	281	32	522
Kansas	103	86	860	51	1100
Kentucky	182	52	322	38	594
Louisiana	113	100	1001	57	1271
Maine	104	9	49	20	182
Maryland	123	9	296	20	448
Massachusetts	812	205	1089	194	2300
Michigan	119	80	462	40	701
Minnesota	504	362	807	114	1787
Mississippi	4	3	201	3	211

STATE	CAMBODIA	LAOS	VIETNAM	OTHER	TOTAL
Missouri	183	133	544	62	922
Montana	4	38	21	6	69
Nebraska	77	22	245	29	373
Nevada	83	18	86	14	201
New Hampshire	67	6	32	16	121
New Jersey	37	35	571	20	663
New Mexico	41	88	222	26	377
New York	835	183	1856	204	3078
North Carolina	94	59	345	30	528
North Dakota	83	10	36	18	147
Ohio	471	167	432	103	1173
Oklahoma	233	94	567	58	952
Oregon	305	322	821	129	1577
Pennsylvania	738	126	1243	154	2261
Rhode Island	153	105	65	47	370
South Carolina	60	40	179	16	295
South Dakota	33	12	67	11	123
Tennessee	186	173	272	68	699
Texas	1204	525	4407	367	6503
Utah	194	167	198	76	635
Vermont	25	6	10	2	43
Virginia	456	79	924	104	1563
Washington	604	587	1352	235	2778
West Virginia	6	26	40	8	80
Wisconsin	39	242	248	40	569
Wyoming	1	0	13	0	14
TOTAL	13051	6914	37085	3977	61027

Note: The data reported in this appendix were obtained from the Center for Disease Control (CDC), as the Office of Refugee Resettlement (ORR) could not provide ethnic and state breakdowns. However, the CDC data were not complete for 1975. They contained only 109,000 records against an ORR figure of 129,792. To resolve this problem, the CDC figures for 1975 were adjusted upward in proportion to their original contribution to the CDC total so that a revised total of 129,792 could be shown. The assumption of this adjustment is that the missing records would be distributed in a manner identical to those that exist.

Appendix B

Indochinese Refugee Needs Assessment Survey (English Version)

Record time begun:

1. What year did you arrive in the United States?

2. In what year did you come to San Diego?

3. Where were you originally resettled when you came to the United States (city and state)?

4. A. How well do you feel you can speak and understand English?
   For example:
   1) Can you read a newspaper in the English language? Yes, no, don't know/no answer
   2) Can you write a letter or fill out a job application in English?
   B.
   1) Can you read in (language being spoken)?
   2) Can you write in (language being spoken)?
   C. What other languages do you speak?
   Can you read in _____? Can you write in _____?

5. Do you own or rent the housing you currently live in?
   (Own house, Rent house, Own apartment, Rent apartment, Own condo, Rent condo, Own or rent other, Rent-free, don't know/no answer)

6. How long have you been living at your current residence?
   (0–3 months, 3–6 months, 6–12 months, 12–18 months, 18–24 months, 24–36 months, more than 3 years, don't know/no answer)

7. How many times have you moved since coming to San Diego?

8. Do you still expect to be living in the San Diego area in two years?
   (yes, no, don't know/no answer)
   If no, why will you be leaving the San Diego area?

9. Do you still expect to be living in the San Diego area in five years?

(yes, no, don't know/no answer)
If no, why will you be leaving the San Diego area?

10. Other than those who live with you in the same house, how many of your relatives, with whom you have frequent contact, live in the San Diego area?

11. Do you have any relatives who live in the United Staes but who are not residing in the San Diego area?
(yes, no, don't know/no answer)
If yes, are any of them planning to move to the San Diego area?
(yes, no, don't know/no answer)

12. A. Counting yourself, how many people live in your house?
B. How many are only living in your house temporarily?

13. Now I'd like you to please tell me the following information about each person who lives with you in the same house, starting with the oldest.
Is this person male or female?
What is his or her age?
What is his or her relationship to you?
Has he or she ever taken or is he or she now taking an ESL course?
If sixteen or older: Has he or she ever had job training in the United States?
If sixteen or older: Is he or she employed?
If sixteen or older: What is his or her job title?
If sixteen or older: How much is he or she paid per hour for that work?

14. About how much do you think the total monthly income is for your household?
(Up to $400 per month, $400–700, $700–1,000, $1,000–1,300, $1,300–1,600, $1,600–1,900, $1,900–2,200, more than $2,200, don't know/no answer)

Now I have a few questions about you.

15. First, what is your age?

16. Are you currently enrolled in an ESL course? (yes, no, don't know/no answer)
If yes, how many months have you been attending ESL?
If no, have you ever attended an ESL class? (yes, no, don't know/no answer)
If yes, how many months did you attend?

17. Have you attended a formal orientation on living in the United States?
(yes, no, don't know/no answer)

18. Are you a member of an Indochinese Mutual Assistance Association (IMAA)?
(yes, no, don't know/no answer)

19. What is your religion?
(Buddhism, Catholicism, Taoism, Protestantism, Confucianism, Hinduism, Moslem, ancestor worship, other [specify], don't know/no answer)

20. Are you married, single, divorced, separated, or widowed?
(question also allows for don't know)
If married, was your spouse able to leave your home country with you?

(yes, no, don't know/no answer)
If no, is your spouse with you in this country now?
(yes, no, don't know/no answer)

21. Were you among the first in your family to settle in this country, or did you come to be reunited with family members who were already here? (among the first, reunited, don't know/no answer)

22. Is there a member of your immediate family who used to live with you and who is now left behind in your home country or in a country other than the United States? (yes, no, don't know where they are, don't know/no answer)

23. What is the main reason you left your home country?

24. In your home country, about how many people lived in the village or city where you spent most of your life? (less than 500, 500–1,500, 1,500–10,000, 10,000–100,000, more than 100,000, don't know/no answer)

25. What is your ethnicity? (Vietnamese, Chinese-Vietnamese, Laotian, Lao H'Mong, Chinese-Lao, Cambodian, Chinese-Cambodian, Other [specify], don't know/no answer)

26. How much formal education or training have you obtained in your home country? How much formal education have you obtained in the United States? (no formal education or training, elementary school or less, some high school, some high school plus trade or commercial school, high school graduate, trade or commercial school beyond high school, some college, no degree, college graduate, master's degree, doctor's degree, other [specify])

27. Do you have a car available for your use? (yes, no, don't know/no answer) If no, do you use the bus for transportation? (yes, no, inappropriate question, don't know/no answer) If not, why not? (probe for specific answer)

28. Not counting the people who live with you, are there any other Indochinese households who use your telephone because they do not have one of their own? (yes, no, don't know/no answer) If yes, how many people are in those households?

29. What was your main occupation in your home country? (never employed, self-employed, Occupation)

30. Are you currently employed? (yes, no, don't know/no answer)

31. Do you have more than one job? (yes, no, inappropriate question, don't know/no answer) If more than one job, ask questions for all jobs.

32. Do you work full-time (35 hours) or part time?
    (full-time, part-time, inappropriate question, don't know/no answer)

33. A. What is your job title?
    B. Are you self-employed?
    (yes, no, inappropriate question, don't know/no answer)
    If yes, do you own your own business?
    (yes, no, inappropriate question, don't know/no answer)
    If yes, note alternatives for this situation in questions.

34. What do you do at your job(s)?

35. How did you find your job(s)?
    (through state employment agency, private employment agency, newspaper ad, friend, service organization, relative, employment prearranged, self, inappropriate question, don't know/no answer, other [probe for specific answer])

36. How long have you been employed at your present job(s)?
    (0–3 months, 3–6 months, 6–12 months, 12–18 months, 18–24 months, 24–36 months, more than 3 years, inappropriate question, don't know/no answer)

37. About how long do you plan to stay at your present job(s)?
    (0–3 months, 3–6 months, 6–12 months, 12–18 months, 18–24 months, 24–36 months, more than 3 years, inappropriate question, don't know/no answer)

38. What do you think would be the main reason you would leave your present job(s)?
    (pay, working conditions, promotion opportunities, overqualified educationally, don't like the work, don't get along with personnel, inappropriate question, don't know/no answer, other [probe for specific answer])

39. About how many people do you work with/employ?
    (number of coworkers, inappropriate question, don't know/no answer)

40. Are all, most, about half, few, or none of the people you work with/employ (respondent's ethnic group)? (In addition to responses named, survey allows for "inappropriate question" and "don't know/no answer.")

41. How do you get to work?
    (car/car pool, bus, walk, bicycle, motorcycle/moped, inappropriate question, don't know/no answer, other [specify])

42. Are you paid by the hour, weekly, or per month? (In addition to responses named, survey allows for "inappropriate question" and "don't know/no answer.")

43. How much are you paid per hour/week/month at your job(s)?

44. Not considering wages or salaries, do you think your current job(s) has more, the same, or is lower in responsibilities than your last job in (respondent's home country)? (In addition to responses named, survey allows for "unsure," "inappropriate question," and "don't know/no answer.")

45. Do you feel satisfied or dissatisfied with your job(s)?
    (satisfied, dissatisfied, inappropriate question, don't know/no answer)
    If dissatisfied, why are you dissatisfied?
    (Pay, working conditions, promotion opportunities, overqualified educationally,
    don't like the work, don't get along with personnel, inappropriate question,
    don't know/no answer, other [probe for specific answer])

46. How many jobs, not including your current one(s), have you had since you
    came to the United States?
    (none other than current job, number of other jobs, inappropriate question,
    don't know/no answer)
    A. Since you first came to San Diego?
    (none other than current job, number of other jobs, inappropriate question,
    don't know/no answer)

47. What did you do at your *last* job?

48. How long were you employed at your last job?
    (0–3 months, 3–6 months, 6–12 months, 12–18 months, 18–24 months,
    24–36 months, more than 3 years, inappropriate question, don't know/no
    answer)

49. Why did you leave that job?
    (pay, working conditions, promotion opportunities, overqualified educationally,
    didn't like the work, didn't get along with personnel, inappropriate question,
    don't know/no answer, other [probe for specific answer])

For the unemployed

50. Have you ever been employed in the United States?
    (yes, no, inappropriate question, don't know/no answer)

51. How many jobs have you had since you first came to the United States?
    (number of jobs, inappropriate question, don't know/no answer)

52. How many jobs have you had since you first came to San Diego?
    (number of jobs, inappropriate question, don't know/no answer)

53. What was your job title at your *last* job?

54. What did you do at your *last* job?

55. How long were you employed at your last job?
    (0–3 months, 3–6 months, 6–12 months, 12–18 months, 18–24 months,
    24–36 months, more than 3 years, inappropriate question, don't know/no
    answer)

56. Why did you leave that job?
    (pay, working conditions, promotion opportunities, overqualified educationally,
    didn't like the work, didn't get along with personnel, inappropriate question,
    don't know/no answer, other [probe for specific answer])

57. Are you currently looking for work?

(yes, no, inappropriate question, don't know/no answer)

58. Is there any reason why you are not able to look for a job?
(yes, no, inappropriate question, don't know/no answer)
If yes, what is the reason?
(illness/disability, child care, transportation, do not speak English, inappropriate question, don't know/no answer, other [probe for specific answer])

59. What kind of special arrangements or help, for example, child care or transportation, would you need in order to work?

Now I have just a few questions about some different programs.

60. Are you aware of any place(s) where you can receive job skills training?
(yes, no, don't know/no answer)
If yes, what are the names of the places?

61. Have you ever received any job skills training while living in the United States?
(yes, no, don't know/no answer)
If yes, how many job training programs have you participated in?
What are the names of the places where you received the training?
What were you trained to do?
Have you ever used this training on a job?
(yes, no)
If no, why not? (probe for specific answer)

62. Are you aware of any places where you can get advice and help in locating a job?
(yes, no)
If yes, what are the names of the places?
Have you ever used their services?
(yes, no, inappropriate question, don't know/no answer)
If yes, was this service successful in finding a job for you?
(yes, no, inappropriate question, don't know/no answer)

63. A. When you *first* arrived in San Diego, who was most helpful to you in:
B. If you needed help *now*, whose assistance would you seek in:
locating housing?
locating a job?
locating medical aid?
learning about day-to-day living in San Diego?

64. Are you an American citizen?
(yes, no, inappropriate question, don't know/no answer)
If no, do you think it would be helpful for you to obtain American citizenship?
(yes, no, inappropriate question, don't know/no answer)

Now I have a few questions to ask you about health care.

65. First, are you currently being treated by a doctor for any medical problems?
(yes, no, don't know/no answer)

66. Are any other members of your immediate family being treated for a medical problem?
    (yes, no, don't know/no answer)

67. Have you ever been admitted to a hospital while living in the United States?
    (yes, no, don't know/no answer)
    If yes, how many days were you in the hospital during your last admission?
    (number of hospital days, inappropriate question, don't know/no answer)

68. During the past three months, about how many times did you go to the doctor's office?
    (number of visits, don't know/no answer)

69. Are you usually able to obtain health care when you need it?
    (yes, no, don't know/no answer)
    If no, what problems have you had obtaining health care?

70. Are you satisfied with the health care you have received?
    (yes, no, never received care, don't know/no answer)

71. Finally, how would you describe your health? Would you say your health is excellent, good, fair, or poor?
    (In addition to responses named, survey allows for "don't know/no answer.")

On another subject . . .

72. What do you find to be *most difficult* about living in the United States?
    (probe for a specific answer)

73. What do you find *most enjoyable* about living in the United States?
    (probe for a specific answer)

Now I would like to ask you a few questions about government social programs. I want you to understand your answers will be held strictly confidential.

74. A. At the present time, are you receiving any of the following?
    B. If no, while living in the United States, have you ever received any of the following?
    General Relief
    AFDC (Aid to Families of Dependent Children)
    IRAP (Refugee Assistance Program)
    SSI/SSP (Supplemental Security Income)
    RCA (Refugee Cash Assistance)
    Food Stamps
    Medi-Cal

75. Finally, here are some important problems that have been expressed by Indochinese refugees during informal conversations. For each problem, I'd like you to tell me how serious you think it is to you and your community—very serious, somewhat serious, or not very serious.
    Not enough money
    Difficulty in understanding the American way of life

English language problem
Painful memories of war and departure from home country
Being separated from family members
Difficulty in getting good food essential to good health
Lack of job skills training programs
Difficulty in practicing religion
Lack of Indochinese support groups
Problems with raising children in American culture
Alcohol or drug problems
Difficulty in getting information needed for day-to-day living
American prejudice against refugees
Poor housing conditions (i.e., too small, poor heating, etc.)
Lack of help in getting a job
Lack of child care services
Transportation problems
Difficulty in dealing with American agencies
Conflict and negative feelings between different refugee groups
Difficulty in communicating with family members and friends in (respondent's home country)

76. Someone from this office may call you again next year to ask you some follow-up questions concerning the Indochinese refugee population in San Diego. In case they are unable to reach you or you move away, is there someone, a relative or friend, we could contact who would know where we could get a hold of you? (yes, no, refuses second contact, don't know/no answer)
   If yes, who is that person? What is their telephone number? What is their address?

77. Will you give me your name in case my office wants to verify that I gave you this interview correctly?

78. Is your telephone number
   (read number on label in front)

79. In thinking over this interview, are there any additional comments you would like to make?

Thank you very much for your cooperation and for your help with this project.

Notes

Immigrants, Refugees, and Resettlement

1. J. J. Mangalam and C. Morgan, *Human Migration: A Guide to Migration Literature in English, 1955–62* (Lexington, Ky.: University of Kentucky Press, 1968).
2. Julian Wolpert, "Migration as an Adjustment to Environmental Stress," *Journal of Social Issues*, vol. 22, no. 4 (1966): 92–102.
3. Jacob Eichenbaum, "A Matrix of Human Movement," *International Migration* 13 (1975): 21–41.
4. William Peterson, "A General Typology of Migration," *American Sociology Review,* vol. 23, no. 3 (1958): 256–66.
5. E. F. Kunz, "The Refugee in Flight: Kinetic Models and Forms of Displacement," *International Migration Review*, vol. 7, no. 2 (1973): 125–46.
6. Smith Hansen and Anthony Oliver-Smith, *Involuntary Migration and Resettlement: The Problems and Responses of Dislocated People* (Boulder, Colo.: Westview Press, 1982).
7. Aristide R. Zolberg, "Contemporary Transnational Migrations in Historical Perspective: Patterns and Dilemmas," in *U.S. Immigration and Refugee Policy*, ed. Mary Kritz (Lexington, Mass.: Lexington Books, 1983).
8. Sheila Avrin McLean, "International Institutional Mechanisms for Refugees," in *U.S. Immigration and Refugee Policy*, ed. Kritz.
9. House Committee on the Judiciary, *Refugee Admission Proposal* (Washington: Government Printing Office, 1981).
10. Ibid.
11. Thayer Scudder and Elizabeth Colson, "From Welfare to Development: A Conceptual Framework for the Analysis of Dislocated People," in *U.S. Immigration and Refugee Policy*, ed. Kritz.
12. Committee on the Judiciary, *Refugee Admission Proposal*.
13. Gene Levine and Colbert Rhodes, *The Japanese American Community* (New York: Praeger Press, 1981).

Prearrival Experiences

1. Virginia Thompson and Richard Adloff, *Minority Problems in Southeast Asia* (Stanford, Calif.: Stanford University Press, 1955).
2. Frank M. LeBar and Adrienne Suddard, eds., *Laos: Its People, Its Society, Its Culture*, 2d ed. (New Haven: Human Relations Area Files, 1967).
3. Arthur J. Dommen, *Conflict in Laos* (New York: Praeger, 1971).
4. Peter Kunstadter, ed, *Southeast Asian Tribes, Minorities, and Nations* (Princeton, N.J.: Princeton University Press, 1967).
5. John Bastin and Harry J. Benda, *A History of Modern Southeast Asia* (Englewood Cliffs, N.J.: Prentice-Hall, 1968).
6. Dommen, *Conflict in Laos.*
7. Louise Holborn, *Refugees: A Problem of Our Time* (New York: Scarecrow Press, 1975).
8. *Far Eastern Economic Review,* vol. 87, no. 1 (3 Jan. 1975): 14.
9. *Far Eastern Economic Review,* vol. 88, no. 21 (23 May 1975): 11.
10. Timothy N. Castle, *Alliance in a Secret War: The United States and the Hmong of Northeastern Laos* (unpublished master's thesis, San Diego State University, 1979); and Dommen, *Conflict in Laos.*
11. G. Linwood Barney, "The Meo of Xieng Khouang Province, Laos," in *Southeast Asian Tribes*, ed. Kunstadter.
12. William R. Geddes, *Migrants of the Mountains* (Oxford: Clarendon Press, 1976).
13. Barney, "The Meo of Xieng Khouang Province."
14. Robert G. Cooper, "Dynamic Tension: Symbiosis and Contradiction in Hmong Social Relations," in *The New Economic Anthropology,* ed. John Clammer (New York: St. Martin's Press, 1978).
15. Geddes, *Migrants of the Mountains,* p. 57.
16. Cooper, "Dynamic Tension."
17. Geddes, *Migrants of the Mountains.*
18. Castle, *Alliance in a Secret War.*
19. David Wurfel, "Indochina: The Historical and Political Background," in *Southeast Asia Exodus: From Transition to Resettlement,* ed. Elliot L. Tepper (Ottowa: Canadian Asian Studies Association, 1980).
20. Ben Kiernan and Chanthou Boua, eds., *Peasants and Politics in Kampuchea 1942–1981* (New York: M. E. Sharpe, 1982).
21. Donald Lancaster, *The Emancipation of French Indochina* (London: Oxford University Press, 1961); and Milton E. Osborne, *Politics and Power in Cambodia: The Sihanouk Years* (Camberwell, Australia: Longman, 1972).
22. Malcolm Caldwell and Lek Tan, *Cambodia in the Southeast Asian War* (New York: Monthly Review Press, 1973).
23. Kiernan and Boua, *Peasants and Politics.*
24. Francois Ponchaud, *Cambodia Year Zero,* trans. Nancy Amphoux (London: Allen Lane, 1978).
25. *Far Eastern Economic Review,* vol. 116, no. 26 (25 June 1982): 8.
26. U.S., Department of State, Bureau for Refugee Programs, *Refugee Reports,* May 1983.

27. Caldwell and Tan, *Cambodia in the Southeast Asian War.*

28. Kiernan and Boua, *Peasants and Politics.*

29. LeBar and Suddard, *Laos;* and Virginia Thompson, *French Indo-China* (New York: Macmillan and Co., 1937).

30. Thomas Hodgkin, *Vietnam: The Revolutionary Path* (New York: St. Martin's Press, 1981).

31. John T. McAlister, Jr., *Vietnam: The Origins of Revolution* (New York: Alfred A. Knopf, 1969).

32. Susan Sheehan, *Ten Vietnamese* (New York: Knopf, 1967).

33. Committee of Concerned Asian Scholars (CCAS), *The Indochina Story* (New York: Random House, 1970).

34. Frances FitzGerald, *Fire in the Lake* (Boston: Little, Brown and Co., 1972).

35. *Far East Economic Review,* 15 October 1982.

36. Georg Simmel, *The Sociology of Georg Simmel* (London: The Free Press of Glencoe, 1950).

37. Thompson and Adloff, *Minority Problems.*

38. Victor Purcell, *The Chinese in Southeast Asia,* 2d ed. (London: Oxford University Press, 1965).

39. Pao-min Chang, "The Sino-Vietnamese Dispute Over the Ethnic Chinese," *The China Quarterly,* June 1982.

Federal Resettlement Policy

1. Gail Paradise Kelly, *From Vietnam to America: A Chronicle of the Vietnamese Immigration to the United States* (Boulder, Colo.: Westview Press, 1977), 19.

2. Health, Education and Welfare Task Force, *Report to the Congress,* 15 March 1976 (Washington: Government Printing Office, 1976), 31.

3. Bruce Grant, *The Boat People: An "Age" Investigation* (Harmondsworth, Eng.: Penguin Books, 1979), 96.

4. Robert P. DeVecchi, "Politics and Policies of 'First Asylum' in Thailand," in *World Refugee Survey 1982* (Washington: U.S. Committee for Refugees, 1983), 23.

5. Ibid.

6. Department of Health and Human Services, *Report to Congress, January 31, 1982* (Washington: Government Printing Office, 1982), 15.

7. Comptroller General, *The Indochinese Exodus: A Humanitarian Dilemma: Report to the Congress by the Comptroller General of the United States,* 24 April 1979 (Washington: U.S. General Accounting Office, 1979), iv.

8. House Committee on the Judiciary, Subcommittee on Immigration, Refugees and International Law, *Testimony of Diane Ahrens, Commissioner, Ramsey County, Minnesota,* 97th Cong., 22 June 1983 (Washington: Government Printing Office, 1983).

9. Kelly, *From Vietnam to America,* 113.

10. "Vietnamese Refugees Find Starting Anew Is Frustrating Ordeal," *Wall Street Journal,* 22 May 1975, 1; and *Time,* 19 May 1975, 9.

11. Kelly, *From Vietnam to America,* 69; and Darrel Montero, *Vietnamese Ameri-*

cans: Patterns of Resettlement and Socioeconomic Adaptation in the United States (Boulder, Colo.: Westview Press, 1979), 29.

12. Kelly, *From Vietnam to America,* 133.
13. Ibid., 136–60.
14. Comptroller General, *The Indochinese Exodus,* 5–20.
15. House Subcommittee on Immigration, Refugees and International Law, *Testimony of Diane Ahrens.*
16. Ibid.
17. Ibid.
18. Ibid.

Subnational Resettlement Policies

1. Linda Gordon, "Southeast Asian Refugees in the U.S.: Dispersal and Concentration" (Paper presented to the Southwest Social Science Association, 17–20 March 1982, San Antonio, Texas).
2. Senate Committee on the Judiciary, Subcommittee on Immigration and Refugee Policy, *Refugee Act Reauthorization,* Hearing, 97th Cong., 2d Sess., 13 September 1982 (Washington: Government Printing Office, 1983), 245.
3. Berkeley Planning Associates, *Study of the State Administration of the Refugee Resettlement Program* (Berkeley, Calif.: Berkeley Planning Associates, 1982).
4. House Committee on the Judiciary, Subcommittee on Immigration, Refugees, and International Law, *Statement of Diane Ahrens, Commissioner, Ramsey County, Minnesota,* 97th Cong., 22 June 1983 (Washington: Government Printing Office, 1983).
5. *Refugee Reports,* vol. 4, no. 8–9 (18 Nov. 1983).
6. Ibid.
7. House Committee on the Judiciary, Subcommittee on Immigration, Refugees, and International Law, *Statement of John Townsend, State Coordinator, Texas,* 97th Cong., 22 and 28 April 1983 (Washington: Government Printing Office, 1983).
8. Berkeley Planning Associates, *Study of the State Administration.*
9. Ibid.
10. Texas, Department of Human Resources, *Comprehensive Service Plan for Texas FY81–83* (Austin, Tex.: Department of Human Resources, 1981).
11. Washington, Department of Social Services, Bureau of Refugee Assistance, *Washington State Refugee Social Services Delivery Plan FY84* (Olympia, Wash.: Department of Social Services, 1984).
12. Washington, Department of Social Services and Health Services, *Refugee Assistance Termination Study and 10–Month Follow-up* (Olympia, Wash.: Department of Social Services, 1983).
13. Illinois, Department of Public Aid, *Illinois Refugee Resettlement Plan FY82* (Chicago: Department of Public Aid, 1982).

Living Conditions and Adjustment

1. Christine R. Finnan, *Southeast Asian Refugee Resettlement at the Local Level: The Role of the Ethnic Community and Nature of Refugee Impact* (Menlo Park, Calif.: SRI International, November 1983), 27.
2. Ibid., 28.
3. Terry Dunnigan, "Segmentary Kinship in an Urban Society: The Hmong of St. Paul-Minneapolis," *Anthropology Quarterly*, vol. 55, no. 3 (July 1982): 126–38.
4. U.S., House of Representatives, Committee on the Judiciary, *Refugee Admission Proposal* (Washington: Government Printing Office, 1981), 83–84.
5. Ibid., 106–108.
6. Darrel Montero, *Vietnamese Americans: Patterns of Resettlement and Socio-Economic Adaptation in the United States* (Boulder, Colo.: Westview Press, 1979), 67–70.
7. Kathleen McInnis, "Secondary Migration Among Indochinese," *Journal of Refugee Resettlement*, vol. 1, no. 3 (May 1981): 36–43.
8. Ibid., 38.

Health Status and Utilization

1. Roy V. Erickson and Giao Ngo Hoang, "Health Problems among Indochinese Refugees," *American Journal of Public Health*, vol. 70, no. 9 (1980): 1003–1006.
2. Diana Hull, "Migration, Adaptation, and Illness: A Review," *Social Science and Medicine*, vol. 13A, no. 1 (1979): 25–36.
3. John L. Fiedler, "A Review of the Literature on Access and Utilization of Medical Care with Special Emphasis on Rural Primary Care," *Social Science and Medicine*, vol. 15C, no. 3 (1981): 129–37.
4. Fredric D. Wolinsky and Marty Zusman, "Toward Comprehensive Health Status Measures," *The Sociological Quarterly*, vol. 21, no. 4 (1980): 607–21.
5. Thomas T. H. Wan and Scott J. Soifer, "Determinants of Physician Utilization," *Journal of Health and Social Behavior*, vol. 15, no. 2 (1974): 100–112; and Ronald Anderson and Lu Ann Aday, "Access to Medical Care in the U.S.: Realized and Potential," *Medical Care*, vol. 16, no. 7 (1975): 533–46.
6. John C. Hershey, Harold S. Luft, and John M. Gianaris, "Making Sense Out of Utilization Data," *Medical Care*, vol. 13, no. 10 (1975): 838–54.
7. Richard Tessler, David Mechanic, and Margaret Dimond, "The Effect of Psychological Distress on Physician Utilization: A Prospective Study," *Journal of Health and Social Behavior*, vol. 17, no. 4 (1976): 353–64; and George L. Maddox, "Some Correlates of Differences in Self-Assessment of Health Status among the Elderly," *Journal of Gerontology*, vol. 17, no. 2 (1962): 180–85.
8. Angus Campbell, Paul E. Converse, and W. L. Rodgers, *The Quality of American Life: Perceptions, Evaluations, and Satisfactions* (New York: Russell Sage Foundation, 1976).
9. F. C. Nall and J. Speilberg, "Social and Cultural Factors in the Responses of Mexican-Americans to Medical Treatment," *Journal of Health and Social Behavior*, vol. 8, no. 4 (1973): 299–308.

10. Hull, "Migration, Adaptation, and Illness."

11. Richard Tessler and David Mechanic, "Psychological Distress and Perceived Health Status," *Journal of Health and Social Behavior*, vol. 19, no. 3 (1978): 254–62.

12. Sidney Cobb, "Social Support as a Moderator of Life Stress," *Psychosomatic Medicine*, vol. 38, no. 5 (1976): 301–14.

13. Paul Starr et al., "Stressful Life Events and Mental Health among Vietnamese Refugees: Innoculation and Synchronization?" (Paper presented at the Southern Sociological Society, 29 March 1980).

14. Alfred Yankauer, "Refugees, Immigrants and the Public Health," *American Journal of Public Health*, vol. 72, no. 1 (1982): 12–14.

15. Reed Geertsen et al., "A Reexamination of Suchman's Views on Social Factors in Health Care Utilization," *Journal of Health and Social Behavior*, vol. 16, no. 2 (1975): 226–37.

16. James G. Anderson, "Demographic Factors Affecting Health Service Utilization: A Causal Model," *Medical Care*, vol. 11, no. 2 (1973): 104–20; and Lee A. Crandall and R. Paul Duncan, "Attitudinal and Situational Factors in the Use of Physician Services by Low Income Persons," *Journal of Health and Social Behavior*, vol. 22, no. 1 (1981): 64–77.

17. Edward Suchman, "Health Orientation and Medical Care," *American Journal of Public Health*, vol. 56, no. 1 (1966): 97–105; and Diana B. Dutton, "Explaining the Low Use of Health Services by the Poor: Costs, Attitudes or Delivery Systems?" *American Sociological Review*, vol. 43, no. 3 (1978): 348–68.

18. Tran M. Tung, "The Indochinese Refugees as Patients," *Journal of Refugee Resettlement*, vol. 1, no. 1 (1980): 53–60.

19. John M. Goering and Rodney M. Coe, "Cultural Versus Situational Explanations of Medical Behavior of the Poor," *Social Science Quarterly*, vol. 51, no. 2 (1970): 312–19; and Ronald Anderson et al., "Access to Medical Care among the Hispanic Population of the Southwestern United States," *Journal of Health and Social Behavior*, vol. 22, no. 1 (1981): 78–89.

20. Susan J. Welch, John Comer, and Michael Steinman, "Some Social and Attitudinal Correlates of Health Care among the Hispanic Population of the Southwestern United States," *Journal of Health and Social Behavior*, vol. 14, no. 3 (1973): 205–13; and Jerry L. Weaver and Lloyd T. Inui, "Information about Health Care Providers among Low-Income Minorities," *Inquiry*, vol. 12, no. 4 (1975): 330–43.

21. Virginia C. Kennedy, "Rural Access to Regular Source of Medical Care," *Journal of Community Health*, vol. 4, no. 3 (1979): 199–203.

22. Eva J. Salber et al., "Utilization of Services for Preventable Disease: A Case Study of Dental Care in a Southern Rural Area of the United States," *International Journal of Epidemiology*, vol. 7, no. 2 (1978): 163–73.

23. T. W. Bice et al., "Economic Class and the Use of Physician Services," *Medical Care*, vol. 11, no. 4 (1973): 287–96.

Education and Language

1. Robert Wright, "Voluntary Agencies and the Resettlement of Refugees," *International Migration Review* 15 (1981): 157.
2. Leonard Dinnerstein and David M. Reimers, *Ethnic Americans: A History of Immigration and Assimilation* (New York: Dodd, Mead, 1975).
3. Allene Grognet, "Refugees and the English Language: A Crucial Interface," *Journal of Refugee Resettlement*, vol. 1, no. 4 (Aug. 1981): 43–50.
4. Ibid., 48.
5. Christine Finnan, *Southeast Asian Refugee Resettlement at the Local Level: The Role of the Ethnic Community and the Nature of Refugee Impact* (Menlo Park, Calif.: SRI International, Nov. 1983).
6. Ibid., 184.
7. Kang-ning Chan, "Education for Chinese and Indochinese," *Theory and Practice*, vol. 20, no. 1 (1981): 31–44.
8. Grognet, "Refugees and the English Language," 49.
9. R. Marsh, "Socioeconomic Status of Indochinese Refugees in the United States: Progress and Problems," *Social Security Bulletin* 43 (1980): 11.
10. John Schumann, "Social Distance as a Factor in Second Language Acquisition," *Language Learning* 26 (1976): 135.
11. S. Krashen, "Formal and Informal Linguistic Environments in Language Acquisition and Language Learning," *TESOL Quarterly* 10 (1976): 157–67; and H. Kleinmann and James Daniel, "Indochinese Resettlement: Language Education and Social Services," *International Migration Review* 15 (1981): 241–45.
12. "The Essential Contributions of Formal Instruction in Adult Second Language Learning," *TESOL Quarterly* 9 (1975): 173.
13. Kleinmann and Daniel, "Indochinese Resettlement."

Employment

1. J. G. Anderson, "Demographic Factors Affecting Health Service Utilization: A Causal Model," *Medical Care* 11 (1973): 104.
2. Robert L. Bach, "Employment Characteristics of Indochinese Refugees: January 1979," *Migration Today*, vol. 8, no. 3 (1980): 10–14.
3. Robert E. March, "Socioeconomic Status of Indochinese Refugees in the United States: Progress and Problems," *Social Security Bulletin*, vol. 43, no. 10 (Oct. 1980): 11–20.
4. Robert L. Bach and Jennifer B. Bach, "Employment Patterns of Southeast Asian Refugees," *Monthly Labor Review*, vol. 103, no. 10 (Oct. 1980): 31–38.
5. A large part of this analysis is taken from an article written by one of the authors: Paul Strand, "Employment Predictors among Indochinese Refugees," *International Migration Review* 18 (1984): 50–59.
6. March, "Socioeconomic Status of Indochinese Refugees."

The Assimilation Process

1. Stephen Steinberg, *The Ethnic Myth: Race, Ethnicity and Class in America* (New York: Atheneum, 1981), 44.

2. John Goldlust and Anthony H. Richmond, "A Multivariate Model of Immigrant Adaptation," *International Migration Review* 8 (1974): 195.

3. Henry Pratt Fairchild, *The Melting-Pot Mistake* (Boston: Little, Brown and Company, 1926).

4. Senate Committee on the Judiciary, *Review of U.S. Refugee Resettlement Programs and Policies*, Report, 96th Cong., 1st Sess., July 1979 (Washington: Government Printing Office, 1979).

5. S. N. Eisenstadt, *The Absorption of Immigrants* (Westport, Conn.: Greenwood Press, 1975), 10.

6. E. F. Kunz, "The Refugee in Flight: Kinetic Models and Forms of Displacement," *International Migration Review*, vol. 7, no. 2 (1973): 130.

7. Smith Hansen and Anthony Oliver-Smith, eds., "Introduction," *Involuntary Migration and Resettlement: The Problems and Responses of Dislocated People* (Boulder, Colo.: Westview Press, 1982), 2.

8. Ibid., 3.

9. Milton M. Gordon, *Assimilation in American Life* (New York: Oxford University Press, 1964).

10. Lawrence H. Fuch, "Immigration, Pluralism and Public Policy: The Challenge of the Pluribus to the Unum," in *U.S. Immigration and Refugee Policy*, ed. Mary Kritz (Lexington, Mass.: Lexington Books, 1983), 300.

11. James A. Pisarowicz and Vicki Tosher, "Vietnamese Refugee Resettlement: Denver, Colorado 1975–1977," in *Involuntary Migration and Resettlement*, ed. Hansen and Oliver-Smith.

12. Gene Levine and Colbert Rhodes, *The Japanese American Community* (New York: Praeger Press, 1981).

13. C. Michael Lanphien, "Refugee Resettlement: Models in Action," *International Migration Review*, vol. 17, no. 1 (1983): 22–23.

14. Ibid., 25.

15. Levine and Rhodes, *The Japanese American Community*.

16. Darrel Montero, *Vietnamese Americans: Patterns of Resettlement and Socioeconomic Adaptation in the United States* (Boulder, Colo.: Westview Press, 1979).

17. Levine and Rhodes, *The Japanese American Community*.

18. David Haines, "Southeast Asian Refugees in the United States: An Overview," *Migration Today*, vol. 11, nos. 2–3 (1983): 10–13.

19. David Haines, Dorothy Rutherford, and Patrick Thomas, "Family and Community among Vietnamese Refugees," *International Migration Review*, vol. 15, no. 1 (1981): 310–19.

20. Christine Finnan, "A Community Affair: Occupational Assimilation of Vietnamese Refugees," *Journal of Refugee Resettlement*, vol. 1, no. 1 (1980): 8–14; Frank M. LeBar, Gerald C. Hickey, and John K. Musgrave, *Ethnic Groups of Mainland Southeast Asia* (New Haven, Conn.: Human Relations Area Files, 1964);

H. A. Bernatzik, *Akha and Meau* (New Haven, Conn.: Human Relations Area Files, 1947); and William R. Geddes, *Migrants of the Mountains* (Oxford: Clarendon Press, 1976).

21. F. M. Savina, *Histoires des Miao*, 2d ed. (Hong Kong: Société des Missions Etrangères, 1930); Yang Dao, "Why Did the Hmong Leave Laos?," in *The Hmong in the West*, ed. Bruce T. Downing and Douglas P. Olney (Minneapolis: Center for Urban and Regional Studies, University of Minnesota, 1982); and Cheu Thao, "Hmong Migration and Leadership in Laos and in the United States," in *The Hmong in the West*, ed. Downing and Olney.

22. William Theodore de Bary, ed., *Sources of Indian Tradition* (New York: Columbia University Press, 1959).

23. Alan Broderick, *Little Vehicle: Cambodia and Laos* (London: Hutchinson, 1949); and Charles Keyes, *The Golden Peninsula: Culture and Adaptation in Mainland Southeast Asia* (New York: Macmillan Publishing Company, 1977).

24. Lucien Stryk, *The World of Buddha* (New York: Anchor Books, Doubleday, 1969); Broderick, *Little Vehicle*; de Bary, *Sources of Indian Tradition*; and *The Golden Peninsula*.

Policy Assessments and Recommendations

1. Department of Health and Human Services, Office of Refugee Resettlement, "Comparison of Total Ceilings to Total Actual Arrivals of U.S. Refugee Admissions Since FY80," *Refugee Reports*, IV(16), August 12, 1983, 2.

2. House Committee on the Judiciary, Subcommittee on Immigration, Refugees and International Law, *Refugee Assistance*, Hearing, 98th Cong., 1st Sess., 7 June 1983 (Washington: Government Printing Office, 1983), 84.

3. Ibid.

4. Department of Health and Human Services, Office of Refugee Resettlement, *Refugee Resettlement Program: Report to the Congress* (Washington: Office of Refugee Resettlement, 31 January 1983), 13.

5. House Committee on the Judiciary, Hearings, 97th Cong., 1st Sess., 29 September 1981 (Washington: Government Printing Office, 1981), 106.

6. Berkeley Planning Associates, *Study of the State Administration of the Refugee Resettlement Program: Final Report* (Berkeley, Calif.: Berkeley Planning Associates, 28 September 1982).

7. Ibid.

8. Office of Refugee Resettlement, *Refugee Resettlement Program*, 13.

Index